The New Century Pocket Guide for Writers

THIRD EDITION

D0222455

Christine A. Hult
Utah State University

Thomas N. Huckin
University of Utah

Longman

New York   Boston   San Francisco
London Toronto Sydney Tokyo Singapore Madrid
Mexico City Munich Paris Cape Town Hong Kong Montreal

Senior Sponsoring Editor: Virginia L. Blanford
Marketing Manager: Susan Stoudt
Production Manager: Savoula Amanatidis
Project Coordination, Text Design, and Electronic Page Makeup: Nesbitt Graphics, Inc.
Cover Design Manager: John Callahan
Cover Designer: Base Art Co.
Senior Manufacturing Buyer: Alfred C. Dorsey
Printer and Binder: Courier Corporation—Westford
Cover Printer: Lehigh-Phoenix Color Corporation

Library of Congress Cataloging-in-Publication Data

Hult, Christine A.
  The new century pocket guide for writers / Christine A. Hult, Thomas N.
Huckin. — 3rd ed.
    p. cm.
  ISBN 0-205-66109-2
1. English language—Rhetoric—Handbooks, manuals, etc. 2. English
language—Grammar—Handbooks, manuals, etc. 3. Report writing—Handbooks,
manuals, etc. I. Huckin, Thomas N. II. Title.
PE1408.H689 2009
808'.042—dc22

                          2008049654

Longman
is an imprint of

www.pearsonhighered.com

ISBN-13: 978-0-205-66109-1
ISBN-10: 0-205-66109-2

1 Drafting and Revising

Novice and experienced writers tend to devote different amounts of time and attention to preparing to write. Novice writers often dive right into drafting a final version of their papers. Rather than experimenting, inventing, and planning, they spend most of their time struggling with the writing itself. Many experienced writers, however, spend a great deal of time thinking about what they want to say before they actually begin to write. Learn from these experienced writers—take time to prepare prior to drafting.

http://writing.colostate.edu/guides
An introduction to various elements of the writing process

WebLink

Your computer can help you with all stages of the writing process. You will learn different tips and techniques for composing and revising throughout this chapter.

1a Invent and prewrite

Writing begins with thinking. The words that appear on your computer screen are the result of the thinking you do prior to and during the writing process. In the prewriting stage, you invent or discover what you want to say about your subject. As the words *invent* and *discover* imply, during this period you delve into your subject, come up with new ideas, connect these new ideas with prior experiences and knowledge, read about and research your subject, and generally allow your thoughts to take shape.

❶ Brainstorming

Brainstorming refers to generating random ideas or fragments of thought about a topic. You are probably familiar with brainstorming from writing classes you have taken in the past. It is possible to brainstorm as a group, calling out ideas to the instructor, who writes them on the blackboard; at a computer, either individually or with another classmate; or in your writing journal.

❷ Freewriting

Freewriting is related to brainstorming in that it involves writing down thoughts as they come to mind. However, unlike brainstorming, freewriting is typically formulated in connected sentences rather than lists. The idea is to write rapidly in an informal style without conscious regard to details of usage, spelling, and punctuation. It is possible to freewrite with pen and paper or at the computer. Using either your word-processing program or a writing journal, you can freewrite on a topic to generate ideas and to discover information stored in your mind.

❸ Invisible writing

Invisible writing is a computer freewriting technique designed to release you from the inhibitions created by seeing your own words on the computer screen. Compulsive revisers find it difficult to ignore the errors they see on the screen and so are unable to write freely at the computer. When you turn off your monitor and write invisibly, your words do not appear on the screen, so you are free to generate ideas without interruption. You can concentrate on the emerging thoughts rather than on the form those thoughts are taking.

❹ Clustering

Clustering is a prewriting technique that can help you see relationships among the ideas you have generated in brainstorming or freewriting exercises. You begin a clustering session by putting your topic, in the form of a word or a phrase, in the middle of a sheet of paper. Then write down near your topic other words or phrases that come to mind, connecting related ideas or subtopics with lines. When you cluster, you free-associate from one word or phrase to another, allowing your mind to trigger related ideas that may not have occurred to you before.

❺ Debating

Debating is a prewriting technique that can help you explore a controversial issue from all sides. You might begin by writing down all the generalizations you can think of about the topic—either handwriting them in your journal or typing them into a computer file.

If you generate your lists of generalizations using a word-processing program, you can add to, delete, replace, and rearrange the information. The general statements and evidence you accumulate while debating the topic can be used to start an outline or an exploratory draft of your paper.

1b   Gather information but avoid plagiarism

Particularly if your assignment is to write a research paper, you will need to supplement whatever prewriting techniques you use with information gathered from external sources. The ideas you read about and formulate will lead you into a more systematic and extensive search that is focused on a specific topic. If your writing task involves a significant research component, refer to Chapters 2, 3, and 4 for guidance.

There are several informal ways you can begin to gather information for your paper. You can perform a *Google* search on your topic using a variety of search terms. You can discuss your ideas with classmates, friends, family members, and professors who may be able to provide you with information. Browsing through current periodicals in the library will tell you whether your topic is being actively discussed in the media. As you begin your informal, preliminary research on a topic, you will also want to begin taking notes, keeping careful track of your sources to avoid plagiarism (see Chapter 3).

1c   Develop and refine your thesis

Once you have explored your topic, done some prewriting, and consulted a few sources, you are ready to begin thinking about a logical order in which to present the ideas you have developed. No matter how good your information, if your paper is not organized, your readers will not be able to understand what you are trying to say.

❶ Narrowing your focus

Through prewriting, you develop an awareness of what you know and do not know about a topic. As you look back at your prewriting, think about ways in which you could narrow your topic to a manageable size. Try to write one sentence that defines your specific, narrow topic.

❷ Formulating a working thesis statement

Once you have written down your narrow topic, try to state in one or two sentences the main point you want to make about that topic. This will be your working thesis statement. A **thesis statement** concisely identifies the topic and main point of a piece of writing.

❸ Evaluating and revising your working thesis

You may need to revise your working thesis several times as you draft your paper. This is why it is called a "working thesis": it can be clarified, modified, or even completely rewritten during the course of your writing process. Allow your thesis to evolve with your understanding of the topic.

❹ Organizing your information

There is no one right way to organize material. The most frequently used organizational patterns are chronological (by *time*), visual (by *space*), and logical (*step-by-step*). Logical organization is used most frequently. Some examples include organizing from general to specific, by cause and effect, by classification, using comparison and contrast, and by problem and solution.

❺ Writing an outline

Once you have decided which organizational pattern best suits your working thesis, you may find it useful to construct an outline for your paper. You need not be overly concerned with formal outline structure at this point, unless your teacher stipulates a particular outline format. An outline should serve as a guide as you write, not a constraint that confines and limits your thinking.

1d   Review

When composing your first draft, you use the information and ideas you generated in your prewriting, along with your working thesis and outline. In the composing stage of the writing process, your concern shifts from experimenting with ideas and gathering information to expanding your ideas and structuring them into effective, coherent prose. Review that crucial prewriting information before you begin composing your first draft.

❶ Reviewing your thesis and outline

Next, review your working thesis and outline. Add any new ideas that occurred to you while reading through your prewriting. If you think the main idea has shifted since you wrote your working thesis, rewrite it and adjust your outline accordingly.

❷ Using multiple windows

If you prefer, you can use your prewriting and outline documents for reference and begin composing from scratch in a new document. The WINDOW feature of many word-processing programs allows you to work on two or more documents simultaneously. Multiple windows are useful for keeping track of your ideas as you work—you can keep your prewriting, your outline, and your draft in separate windows. It is also possible to use separate windows to display different parts of your document at the same time. For example, you could insert your thesis into one window and your draft into another.

1e   Draft

When you are ready to begin composing, you can choose from a number of approaches. Two are the building-block technique and the top-down method.

❶ Using the building-block technique

One approach to composing is to create a group of building blocks that you can use to construct your text one piece at a time. Many writers first compose a skeleton of the finished text and then expand it by adding new arguments, supporting examples and evidence, or illustrative details—the "building blocks" of a text. Word processing is particularly effective for this approach. Some writers like to write their central paragraphs—the middle blocks of a text—first and add the introductory blocks and concluding paragraphs later. You can decide which blocks will be easiest and write those blocks first, saving the more difficult parts for last.

❷ Using the top-down method

As an alternative to composing from building blocks, you may prefer to work from the beginning of your paper straight through to the end, thus moving from the top down. You can use your working thesis statement and the corresponding organizational plan to compose in this way. Type or COPY and PASTE your working thesis statement into a new document. With the thesis statement at the top of your screen, begin writing your draft, following the blueprint suggested by your thesis. Remember, your working thesis is just that—working. You can revise it at any time.

❸ Avoiding writer's block

Each writer develops his or her own writing rhythms. It is a good idea to get into the habit of stopping a writing session when you know what comes next; this makes it easier to pick up where you left off when you are ready to continue. However, if you find yourself "blocked" as a writer, set your work aside for a few hours or even a few days. Get up and stretch, grab a cup of coffee or a soft drink before returning to your draft. Do not expect perfection from a first draft. Remember that writing is essentially rewriting; everything you write should undergo extensive revision in a continuous cycle of writing, revising, editing, and writing again.

1f   Collaborate

As you compose, you might find it helpful to collaborate with others, either face to face or via a computer network. In college classes, as in the workforce, writers often work on projects in writing groups or writing teams. Your teammates can serve as a sounding board for your ideas and arguments.

❶ Working with a group

Working with a group may be something you enjoy or something you dread, depending on whether your prior experience with group projects was positive or negative. In some group projects, one or two students may end up feeling that they are doing all the work. In other group projects, a few students may be bossy or controlling rather than cooperative. But if you pay attention to group dynamics and role assignments from the start of your collaborative project, you should do just fine.

❷ Writing collaboratively

Once you have come up with an overall plan of action for your writing project, you can assign specific tasks or roles to group members. In one writing class, each group was assigned the task of developing a Web site on a topic related to cyberspace. The students in each group brainstormed together possibilities for their site, first deciding on the nature of the content their Web site would present and the audience it would address. They each then agreed to write independently a two- to three-page piece that would be incorporated as a page at the site. After that, they assigned each person in the group a specific role, from site Webmaster to site publisher. Because each student knew exactly what his or her contribution would be, group members were able to work together cooperatively.

❸ Collaborating via network

If you are involved in a joint writing project, forming an email discussion group can facilitate collaboration with others in the group. Students collaborating to write material for a Web site they were creating, for example, used a study group address so that they could email the first draft of each Web page to the entire writing group for review. Most email software offers the option INCLUDE EMAIL MESSAGE IN REPLY. That option places the entire message—in this case, the draft of a Web page—into the reply window. Members of the writing group could add their comments and suggestions in capital letters or italics to make them stand out from the draft itself. Or, they can use the "track changes" feature to make editing and revision suggestions. Then, by selecting the REPLY TO ALL option, they could send the reply message to everyone in the group, or by selecting the REPLY TO SENDER option, they could send their reply to only the writer.

You can also use the email software's ATTACHMENT capability to facilitate collaboration with a writing group. This feature allows you to include a document (file) with the email message. In this way, you can send your actual word-processing document to the others in the group for their review. Group members can use the word-processing program's COMMENT feature (found in the INSERT menu) to insert their comments and suggestions for revisions. The paper and the comments can then be sent back to the writer, again as an email attachment.

1g   Revise

Critical reading can highlight problems of focus, coherence, organization, development, tone, and formatting in your paper. Revising involves the tasks of adding to the text, deleting from the text, and rearranging information within the text to fix those problems. Using a word-processing program makes these tasks easy; knowing what to add, delete, and rearrange is the tricky part.

❶ Revising for focus
Revisit your working thesis, and revise it to more accurately reflect the overall point of your text. Then revise each paragraph to ensure that it is focused on only one idea that supports the thesis. Delete any paragraphs that are not related to the thesis.

WebLink

http://www.rpi.edu/web/ writingcenter/revise.html
A list of revision tips and strategies

❷ Revising for coherence
Wherever you notice that sentences do not flow smoothly in your draft, add appropriate transitional words and phrases.

Look particularly at the links between paragraphs. Insert transitions to help the reader follow the flow of the text. Such words or phrases as *however, on the one hand, on the other hand, but*, and *in addition* can help the reader see the relationships between ideas.

❸ Revising for organization

Once you have decided how to improve the organization of your text, use the CUT, COPY, and PASTE commands to move parts of your text. Rearrange the words, sentences, and paragraphs that comprise your text into the most effective order. Be certain that you check for coherence after rearranging.

❹ Revising for development

Your argument is stronger if you include concrete examples or details. If you are writing an informal piece, do not hesitate to add anecdotes or narratives of personal experiences to give life and personality to your writing. If you are writing a formal paper, you can add information from sources that support your arguments.

❺ Revising for tone

In rereading, you may decide that your tone is either too formal or too informal. To revise your tone to be more formal, expand contractions into their full forms, combine some short sentences to make longer sentences, and change informal diction or slang into more formal wording.

❻ Revising for format

To convey your information in a more visual way, you may want to add formatting more commonly found in a brochure or a newsletter. You can import and insert graphics to illustrate your text at appropriate points. Try using different fonts by selecting them from the FORMAT menu. Remember, though, that readability of your text is the most important goal; choose fonts accordingly. (See Chapter 8 for more information on fonts.)

❼ Writing effective openings, closings, and titles

Openings   Writers have very little time in which to grab the reader's attention—usually only a few seconds. That is why a piece's opening, or lead, is so important. But do not let concern over how you will begin become a stumbling block. Many writers find that leaving the opening for the last stages of revision works best. Try out several leads before deciding on the most effective one for your audience and purpose.

Closings or Conclusions   A conclusion usually takes the form of a summary, which points the reader back to the text itself, or speculation, which points the reader outside of the text.

Titles   Because the title is the first thing a reader sees, it must make a good impression. The title also must help the reader anticipate the topic and gain insight into the writer's particular point of view.

 Edit

When editing a text, the writer's goal is to make it easier to read. During revision, the writer concentrates on making the piece focused, organized, and well developed. During editing, the writer concentrates on refining words and sentences and checking grammar and usage for correctness.

 Proofread

Proofreading is the final phase in rewriting. In this stage of the process, writers look closely for distracting punctuation and mechanical errors that will interfere with the reader's understanding. By proofreading after revising and editing, writers can concentrate on details related to manuscript preparation, such as typographical errors, missing words, and irregular spacing, as well as errors in punctuation or spelling that they may have missed in earlier stages.

 Give and receive feedback

In many writing classes, students work together in peer review groups in which they exchange drafts for review, either electronically or in hard copy form. The instructor may also comment on early drafts and make revision suggestions. Students may be asked to take their papers to a writing center, where a tutor will read them and offer suggestions. As a writer, you will find it helpful to receive feedback on your work from a variety of sources. Such feedback allows you to become increasingly sensitive to the needs of your readers.

2   Doing Research and Using the Internet

The process of writing a research paper does not differ markedly from the process of writing an essay. The difference is one of scope. A research paper is longer than most essays and contains more information from external sources; this information is found by doing research.

2a   Become a researcher

The ability to research—that is, to explore a problem systematically—is a crucial skill for an educated person. A researcher is a careful, critical, systematic thinker who goes beyond memorizing facts on a subject to examine the bases on which claims and arguments rest.

http://www.wisc.edu/writing/
Handbook/PlanResearchPaper.html
A site devoted to helping writers of
research papers

WebLink

❶ Understanding the research project

When you begin a research project, first think through what you will need to do. Ask yourself questions such as these:

- What will my purpose be?
- How should I sound as a writer?
- Who will my readers be?
- Where will I get my authority?

The two main types of research are primary research and secondary research. **Primary research** entails generating information or data through processes such as experimenting, interviewing, administering questionnaires, or field observation. **Secondary research** involves finding information in secondary, or published, sources. You need to decide which type or types of research your project demands. Discuss with your instructor the kinds of sources that you should be locating and reading for your research project.

❷ Selecting a specific topic

Once you have chosen a topic that you are interested in researching, you need to narrow that topic to a specific issue. Preliminary library or Web searches can help you pose starting questions that your research will attempt to answer.

❸ Developing a hypothesis

As you work through the research process, seeking answers to your starting questions, you should come up with a hypothesis—a tentative statement of what you anticipate the research will reveal. A working hypothesis specifically describes a proposition that research evidence will either support or disprove.

❹ Developing a search strategy

A search strategy is a plan for proceeding systematically with research. Once you have decided on your starting questions and working hypothesis, you are ready to outline your search strategy. Your first decision will be about the nature of your research. Will you be relying mostly on secondary (library and Internet) research or on primary (field) research?

The goal of a search is to build a working bibliography—a list of possible sources that may eventually be used in the final paper. A working bibliography is typically about twice as long as the final bibliography for a research paper, because many of the sources you identify will turn out not to be applicable to your paper or not to be available in time for you to use in your research.

2b   Make a schedule

If you have never done a research project before, you may be overwhelmed at the thought of such a large and complex task. If you break the job down into smaller parts, however, it will seem much more manageable. It is helpful to formulate a time frame in which to complete your research project. If your instructor has not given you deadlines, set your own dates for accomplishing specific tasks. Give yourself enough time to plan, organize, write a first draft, and make revisions.

2c   Create a research notebook

It is important to create a notebook in which to record all the information relating to your research project. If you are using a word-processing program, you can take advantage of its storage capabilities to develop an electronic research notebook. Create a folder, and label it as your research notebook. In this folder, you can create files or documents to record your topic and your starting questions, notes from your background research and focused research, and your working bibliography (if you do not have bibliography software).

❶ Recording notes in a notebook

Whether the notebook in which you record your notes is handwritten or computer-generated, be sure to keep your recorded notes separate from your comments. If your notebook is handwritten, you might use two columns when recording information: one for notes taken from the source and the other for comments, analyses, and queries. If your notebook is electronic, you can use your word-processing program's DOCUMENT COMMENTS feature to INSERT your comments and analyses into the notes taken from sources.

❷ Taking notes with photocopies, printouts, and downloads

With photocopy machines and computer printers now so readily available in libraries and computer labs, more researchers are making use of these tools to record source information. Making your own photocopies and printouts of sources has many advantages: first, you will have the actual wording of the authors at your fingertips; second, you can highlight passages that are important to your own research for future reference; and third, you can write directly on the photocopies or printouts.

When you are researching on the Internet, it might be easiest for you to print out copies of relevant Web pages rather than taking separate notes. If there is a specific section of a Web page that you wish to use as a source, you can highlight that section using your computer's mouse and then choose PRINT > SELECTION from the PRINT dialog box. In this way, you will print only the parts you need and not the entire Web site. As with photocopies, printouts of sources from the Internet will also need to have complete bibliographic information.

Another method of obtaining information from the Internet is to download or save Internet pages directly into your own computer files (using FILE > SAVE AS). When downloading or copying and pasting files from the Internet, be especially careful not to import source information directly into your own work without citing the source appropriately. To keep from inadvertently plagiarizing from the Internet, take special care to type into your computer notebook the complete bibliographic information from each source and to put quotation marks around any text that is copied and pasted from the Internet. Also, note for yourself the author of the quotation so that you can use that information in a signal phrase that introduces the quotation.

2d   Create a working bibliography

A **bibliography** is a listing of books and articles on a particular subject. When you submit a research paper, you include a bibliography to show readers what sources you consulted to find your information. As you begin your research, start a working bibliography, which will grow as your research progresses. This working bibliography will likely contain some sources that ultimately you will not use in your research paper, so entries need not be in final bibliographic form. However, it is important to record accurately all the information you will need to compose your final bibliography so that you do not have to track down sources twice.

2e   Gather additional background information

Now is the time to gather additional background information, using your starting questions and working hypothesis as a guide. This information will help you conduct more focused research later on.

❶ Starting with yourself

At the start of a research project, write down everything you already know about your topic. The list may be quite extensive or rather short. The important thing is to inventory your own knowledge first so that you can systematically build on that knowledge base. The more you know about your topic, the better you will be at judging the value of sources you read. Also, check your biases and assumptions about the topic.

❷ Doing preliminary background reading in general reference books

We recommend that you begin your library search in the general reference section. Here you will find reference books that have condensed huge amounts of information into an accessible form. These sources can help you define your subject area more clearly, identify keywords and important authors, and gain a general understanding of your topic. Most reference works are available both in book versions and in computerized versions (either on CDs or on the Internet).

2f Conduct focused research

Once background reading has helped you understand your subject, narrow it to a manageable size, and formulate a hypothesis, you are ready to read about your topic in a more focused way. Conducting focused secondary research involves locating the specific information you need to write your paper.

❶ Using the library's online catalog

The computerized catalog is one of the most visible research tools in libraries today (see Figure 2.1). Computerized systems, which have replaced the traditional card catalog, are designed to handle various library functions, such as circulation, cataloging, and location of materials within the library collection. Most computerized catalogs are searchable by author, title, and subject; in addition, computerized catalogs are searchable by keyword or by a combination of subject and keyword. (See Keyword Searching on page 17.)

Typically, a library's computerized catalog indexes books, government documents, and audiovisual materials. The articles that you find in a computerized

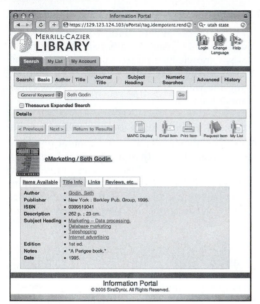

Figure 2.1 ► Library Catalog Entry

catalog search may or may not be available in your own library, as most libraries can afford to subscribe to only a limited number of magazines, newspapers, and journals. If your library does not own a particular magazine, newspaper, or journal, do not despair. Through interlibrary loan or the Internet, often you can locate an article and obtain it for your own use. Check with the librarian to find out about such reciprocal services.

❷ Using the library's online databases to locate journals and magazines

The most reliable way of conducting a search on any academic subject is through your college library's database services. Your library will provide

> ## Keyword Searching
>
> 1. **What is a keyword search for?** A keyword search allows you to search an electronic database for the term or terms that you have identified as being most important for your project.
> 2. **Where does the computer search for the keywords?** The computer will locate all terms in the database that include the particular keywords or terms anywhere in the work's record, from the title to the body to the bibliography.
> 3. **Can the computer supply other related words?** Typically, the computer will not be able to supply synonyms for the keywords you have identified. You need to think of as many keywords as possible.
> 4. **What terms should I use as keywords?** You will have to use your knowledge of the topic, gained through background reading, to come up with keywords. For example, if you are searching the subject of UFOs, you might use *UFO* as a keyword. But you also might want to try *flying saucers* or *paranormal events*.
> 5. **Can I do a keyword search on the Internet?** The same kind of keyword searching discussed here can be done on the Internet.

access to numerous indexes that list sources, as well as to full-text sources on academic subjects. The advantage of searching through your library's databases is that you eliminate a lot of the extraneous "noise" that you get from a *Google* search. If you simply type keywords into *Google*, you will get commercial sites, advertising sites, popular press, personal blogs, and so on. A *Google Scholar* search is better than a general *Google* search, but still it may lead you only indirectly to the full-text databases to which your library subscribes. The best place to start is in your own library.

Types of Databases   Each library organizes its databases differently, so you will need to become acquainted with the system used on your campus. Your reference librarians and any online help system provided at your library's Web site can get you started. For example, at Utah State University,

Figure 2.2 ► Electronic Resources and Databases from the Utah State University Library

the library's opening search screen (Electronic Resources and Databases) provides a full range of information that can be found via the library's Web portal: everything from full-text collections to searches by academic subject, specialized database searches, and encyclopedias and dictionaries (see Figure 2.2).

Keywords   You will first need to make a list of keywords on your topic (see Keyword Searching on p. 17). If you are researching global warming, for example, you want to use all the possible keywords that you can think of—and any others that turn up in your background reading. Find a good all-around database at your library's Web page, such as *Academic Search Premier* (from *EBSCOhost*) or *Lexis-Nexis Academic*. Type in your keywords, using AND to narrow the search or OR to expand the search. Check any limiters you might want, such as searching for the last five years or full-text only.

Keeping Track of Database Sources It is very important to keep track of all the sources you located through a particular database. The Modern Language Association (MLA) documentation system, for example, requires that you list the database through which you located the material. Furthermore, if you ever need to find the article again, you will need to know where it was located. As you browse the titles in the *EBSCOhost* database, you can add them to a folder in which you store all the relevant information from this particular search. Once items are in the folder, you can save to a disk, print, email, or archive those items you wish to retain for future reference.

❸ Using online newspaper databases

Your library will most likely subscribe to full-text newspaper databases as well as other library databases. Check the opening screen of your library's electronic resources page for a link to databases such as *ProQuest Newsstand* or *Utah Digital Newspapers Project*. A search via *ProQuest Newsstand* yielded numerous recent articles on UFOs and paranormal events. It is also possible to search the archives of major newspapers such as the *New York Times*, but such searches often involve a fee for service.

❹ Using other Internet resources

The Internet is becoming an increasingly important research tool in all fields of study. A biologist observed that he can locate information crucial to his research in minutes via the Internet, when it used to take days or even weeks of searching through print sources. See 2g for more on using the Internet for research.

❺ Doing primary, or field, research

In all disciplines, researchers use primary research methods to gather information and search for solutions to problems. Primary research methods include *experimentation*, *observation*, *surveys*, and *interviews*.

Observation The general goal of observation is to describe and perhaps evaluate customary behaviors. Observation is best suited to the collection of nonverbal data. The observer watches people behave in customary ways in a particular environment or setting and takes notes. These "field notes" are used to analyze trends and discern customary behaviors. The disadvantages of observation include lack of control over the environment, lack of quantifiable data, and small sample size.

Surveys Ideally, an entire population would be studied to gain insights into its society. However, polling an entire population is seldom feasible, so surveys are used to sample small segments of the population selected at random. One common kind of survey is the questionnaire, a form that asks for responses to a set of questions. Designing questions is a science that has been developed over the years. The basic principles are to be sure that the questions you write are clear and understandable and are written in such a way that the responses will be easy to tabulate.

Interviews The interview is a particular type of survey. The advantages of the interview include flexibility (the questioner can interact with the respondent), speed of response (the questioner immediately knows the responses), and nonverbal behavior (the questioner can gather nonverbal as well as verbal clues).

2g Use Internet sources throughout the research process

Searching the Internet for information on a topic is similar in many respects to researching in the library. When beginning to research on the Internet, you should follow a search strategy, as outlined in 2a–4. Use the Internet for finding and exploring research topics, for background and focused searching, and even for collaboration with your peers and feedback from your instructor. Email and online discussion forums are ideal tools for trying out your topic ideas on your instructor and peers.

WebLink
http://www.lib.berkeley.edu/TeachingLib/Guides/
Current information on Internet searching, from UC Berkeley librarians

2h Get to know the Internet and the Web

The World Wide Web, a huge spider web–like structure that encompasses computer networks throughout the world, seems to have been woven overnight. But no one spider wove this web; anyone and everyone can contribute (see Chapter 8 for information on designing and writing for the Web).

The Web is by far the easiest and most popular way of accessing information from the Internet. The Web provides a hypertext interface for "reading" Internet information. This means that information is presented in the form of a series of links, each leading to another document or another location on the Internet. Documents structured as text with a series of links to other texts are called hypertexts. One simply uses a mouse to click on the link (usually a graphic or a word or phrase in blue type with blue underlining) to connect with the hyperlinked document. Researchers navigate the Web through the use of an Internet browser.

❶ Surfing the World Wide Web

You will probably be accessing the Internet through a direct connection in a campus computer lab. If you wish to use your personal laptop on campus to access the Internet, it is a good idea to check with your computing center to find out the best way to connect to the campus computer network.

Once you have an Internet connection, you will need an Internet browser in order for your computer to display Web pages. If you are using a computer in a campus lab, there will probably be icons on the opening screen for the two most popular browsers, *Mozilla Firefox* or *Internet Explorer*. They contain comparable features and are free. If you are using a recent version of Windows, you will find that *Internet Explorer* has already been installed on your computer.

❷ Keeping track of your search

Both *Firefox* and *Explorer* help you keep track of important Web sites and retrace the steps of your Internet search. The GO feature keeps a running list of the Web sites you have visited during your current Internet session. It will disappear when you close your browser. To retrace your steps after an Internet search, you can use the HISTORY feature of your browser, found on the toolbar.

If you have found a page that you want to visit frequently, you can add this site's address to your list of bookmarks (*Firefox*) or favorites (*Explorer*). You can add a page to your bookmarks or favorites by visiting that page and then choosing ADD BOOKMARK or ADD TO FAVORITES from the bookmark menu or button.

❸ Respecting copyright and avoiding plagiarism

As a student, you need to be careful to behave ethically and responsibly both when using Web materials and when publishing your own work on the Web. In any piece of writing, including Web pages, be certain that you cite all sources, including Internet sources, in a way that readers can locate them easily. Because it is so easy now to simply copy and paste information from the Internet into your own document files, you need to be especially vigilant. See Chapter 3 for more information about using sources responsibly and avoiding plagiarism.

When writing your own Web pages, also be sure to only download images or texts that are considered "freeware," offered by the site to users free of charge. If you are not certain, you should email the author or site sponsor for permission to either download the material or link to it from your own page.

2i   Search the Internet and the Web

Many corporations, nonprofit organizations, and special-interest groups maintain information-rich Web sites. The purposes of these sites vary from disseminating information to peddling propaganda to luring customers into spending money. When you use information from an Internet source, remember that unless it is part of a well-known professional organization's site, it probably has not been reviewed by anyone other than members of the organization that maintains the site, and so its objectivity may be questionable.

❶ Using search tools to locate information

How do you go about finding specific information on a particular topic? The most reliable way is to use one of the Internet search tools. Search tools use different methods of sorting Web pages. Some search tools, often called search engines, use an automated system to sort pages based primarily on the use and placement of keywords. *Google* and *Yahoo!* are examples of search engines. Search engines automatically find and catalog new sites as they are added to the Web, indexing information by title and keywords.

❷ Searching with keywords

Once you have selected a search engine, you need to determine what search terms to try. Enter a keyword that identifies your topic, and search for hits of that keyword—Web pages on which the word appears.

❸ Using Boolean operators

One way search tools allow you to narrow your search is by means of Boolean operators, which allow you to expand or limit searches with words such as *AND* or *NOT*. It is best to use capital letters with these words since some search engines require it. Learning to search the Internet and the Web effectively will help you become a better researcher.

3 Evaluating and Using Sources: Avoiding Plagiarism

Writers gain credibility through the use of information from experts. It is the responsibility of research authors to be certain that any information from another author, whether paraphrased, summarized, or quoted, is accurately relayed and clearly acknowledged. Integrating source information into one's own writing is a skill that takes practice.

3a   Choose legitimate sources

Because you will be relying on your sources to provide the evidence and authority to support your hypothesis, it is crucial that you choose legitimate sources. Your reputation as a researcher may be at stake. Decide whether the source is worth using by considering its relevance; the publisher or sponsor of the source; the author of the material; the timeliness of the piece; and whether this source is cited or cross-referenced in any other works.

For a Web site, look at the domain type to find out some information about the sponsor of the site. These are some common domain types:

- Education (.edu)
- Government (.gov)
- Nonprofit organization (.org)

- Commercial (.com)
- Network (.net)
- Military (.mil)
- Other countries (.ca for Canada; .uk for United Kingdom)

Being careless about your sources can lead to a serious academic offense called plagiarism—with serious consequences such as a failing grade for the course or even expulsion from school. **Plagiarism** is defined as the unauthorized or misleading use of the language and text of another author. Whenever you use exact words from a source, this must be indicated clearly through the use of a signal phrase, quotation marks, and an in-text citation at the point in the text where the source information is quoted. Readers must be able to tell as they are reading your paper exactly what information came from which source and what information is your own contribution to the paper. (See 3c.)

Use sources responsibly

When writing a research paper, you must acknowledge any original information, ideas, and illustrations that you find in another author's work, whether it is in print or on the Internet. Acknowledging the work of other authors is called documenting sources. (The appropriate forms for documentation are discussed in Chapters 6 and 7.)

http://www.wisc.edu/writing/
Handbook/QuotingSources.html
Detailed explanations and
examples of using quotations,
paraphrases, and summaries

3c   Avoid plagiarism

If you use source information carefully and accurately, you will avoid any charges of plagiarism. By following the guidelines in this chapter when you paraphrase, summarize, and quote, you will never plagiarize.

Acknowledgment Required   Any word, phrase, or sentence that you copied directly from a source must be placed in quotation marks, and complete bibliographic information must be given, including the page reference for the quotation. Similarly, you must acknowledge paraphrases and summary restatements of ideas taken from a source, even though you have cast them in your own words.

No Acknowledgment Required   You need not document "common knowledge." This term refers to information that is generally known or accepted by educated people. Information that you can find readily in general reference works such as encyclopedias or in the popular media is probably common knowledge and need not be documented, although it must be stated in your own words. Proven historical facts and dates need not be documented.

Unintentional Plagiarism   Your notes should accurately record source information in your own words. You should be able to tell at a glance from your notes when information is from a source and when it is your own commentary or thoughts on a source. Students taking notes from a source sometimes commit *unintentional* plagiarism by carelessly copying words and phrases from a source into their notes and then using these words and phrases without acknowledgment in a paper.

Intentional Plagiarism   Sometimes plagiarism is *intentional*; that is, a writer knowingly copies the work of another without proper acknowledgment of the source. Whenever you use words from a source, this must be indicated clearly through the use of quotation marks and documentation at the point in the text where the source information is used. It is not enough to list the author in the footnotes or bibliography. Readers must be able to tell as they are reading your paper exactly what information came from which source and what information is your contribution to the paper. That way, they can follow your research trail and form their own judgments.

3d   Paraphrase sources accurately

Instead of directly quoting from sources, writers have the option of **paraphrasing** source information. The objective of paraphrasing is to present an author's ideas clearly, using your own words and phrases instead of quoting the author. This important skill not only deepens your understanding of the author's ideas but also helps you avoid plagiarism.

With paraphrases, as with quotations, you must indicate on what page in the source you found the information. Ideally, anyone else reading your work should be able to locate the exact wording from which your paraphrase was taken.

3e   Summarize sources briefly

Summaries condense the information found in sources. Like paraphrasing, summarizing involves restating the author's ideas or information in your own words, but summaries are typically much briefer than the original information. The goal of a summary is to record the gist of the piece—its primary line of argument—without tangential arguments, examples, and other departures from the main ideas. As with paraphrasing, you need to be sure that the summary is stated in your own words.

❶ Recording summaries in notes

When you first preview a source to determine its relevance to your research, you can also decide how much of the source you are likely to use in your paper. You would not want to paraphrase an entire article, for example, if only the introduction related to your topic. Rather, you could simply summarize the relevant portion.

❷ Integrating summaries into a paper

Summaries are incorporated into a paper in much the same way as direct quotations and paraphrases. Introduce a summary with a signal phrase, place it in a context for the readers, or perhaps use the author's name or article title in the introduction. As with quoting and paraphrasing, you need to provide documentation indicating the source of the summarized information.

❸ Avoiding plagiarism when summarizing

Using your own words and providing documentation for the source will produce a summary that avoids plagiarism. A summary that uses the same wording and sentence structure of the original source and that fails to provide documentation may be plagiarism.

3f   Quote sources sparingly

Quotations are exact wordings taken from sources. Use direct quotations sparingly in a research paper. A string of quotations can be confusing for readers, especially if each presents information in a different writing style. By paraphrasing and summarizing instead of quoting, you can more smoothly incorporate the ideas from sources into your own writing. However, if an author uses unique language or an interesting image, a brief quotation may be an effective addition to a paper.

❶ Using quoted material

When you quote from a source, it is important to be accurate. Making photocopies or printouts of a source can help you quote exactly because you can check the wording against the original. Every time you copy information from a source, indicate through quotation marks in your notes that you have taken the exact wording from the original.

❷ Integrating quotations into a paper

When you use a direct quotation, you must integrate it smoothly into the flow of your ideas. Use signal phrases to alert your reader that a quotation is coming. Be sure to attribute the source appropriately (see Chapters 6 and 7 on documentation formats) and punctuate it correctly (see Chapter 21 on quotation marks). The quotations that you use should be relatively short to minimize interruption.

4   Writing the Research Paper

Now that you have gathered and evaluated your information, you need to step back and assess just where all this research has taken you. Although the process that you will follow in writing your research paper is not radically different from the writing process outlined earlier in this handbook, there are some important differences. The first difference is one of scope: a research paper is longer than most essays. Sometimes students find themselves overwhelmed by the sheer volume of information they have collected. It is indeed a huge challenge to organize and present research.

4a   Review your purpose, audience, and thesis

Remind yourself of your intended purpose for writing the research paper. Ask yourself, "Who is my audience?" You may not be able to determine for certain who your readers will be, but you can assume that they will be intelligent people who have an interest in the topic you are writing about. It is unlikely that they will be experts in the field you are discussing; therefore, you should define any terms carefully and avoid using jargon or technical vocabulary.

❶ Writing a thesis statement

A thesis statement for a research paper is similar to a thesis statement for an essay. That is, it states for readers the central idea that the paper will argue. Many times, the working thesis statement is revised during the actual writing process.

❷ Revising the thesis

Most research papers argue a position. However, some research papers are informational; that is, they report on information without taking a position. Your teacher may require that your thesis (and hence your research paper) have an argumentative edge. If so, make sure that you have taken a stand that can be supported through arguments in the paper.

❸ Deciding on a voice and tone

Academic papers should be informative and serious, but they need not be dull or dry. You can still put your own personality into a piece. Although it is generally not appropriate to adopt too informal a tone for an academic research paper, taking yourself out of the piece entirely may leave readers with the impression that the piece is lifeless and uninteresting. Try to strike a balance in your tone, making it pleasing to readers.

4b   Plan a structure

Some writers like to work from an organizational plan or outline, fleshing out the skeleton by incorporating additional information under each of the major points and subpoints. Others prefer to begin writing and have the structure evolve more organically. You need not be overly concerned about formal structure at this point unless your teacher stipulates a particular outline format.

4c   Write a draft

Now you should be ready to begin drafting your research paper. Remind yourself of your general understanding of the topic, your starting questions and hypothesis, and the answers to the questions as stated in your thesis. When writing your first draft, use concrete and simple language to explain your research conclusions in your own words. Ideally, you should type your draft on a computer to make revisions easier.

❶ Choosing a drafting strategy

You will need to establish your own strategy for writing a first draft, one that fits your writing style. Here are a few ways in which writers of research projects proceed:

- Write a draft systematically from a plan, using the building-block technique (see 1e-1).
- Write a draft using the top-down method (see 1e-2).
- Write a rough first draft, and then write a revision outline that suggests ways in which the draft needs to be changed.
- Write a draft using your photocopied or printed sources (2c-2).

❷ Applying the drafting strategy to blend material

As you draft, you blend your own knowledge with material from sources. In writing a first draft, it is best to put down your own understanding of the topic first, rather than relying too heavily on your sources. After you have written your draft, you can go back and add specific sources to support your arguments. Readers want to know what *you* think about the subject. They do not want to read a string of quotations loosely joined by transitions.

❸ Writing the introduction and conclusion

Composing introductions and conclusions is discussed in 1g-7. Because a research paper typically covers more information than an essay, it may take a couple of paragraphs to introduce the topic effectively. You should make certain that both your introduction and your conclusion help readers understand your research paper's main point.

4d   Review and revise the draft

A great deal of important work remains to be done on your paper once you complete a rough draft. You must revise the paper to make the most effective possible presentation of the research. Readers expect you to be clear and correct; they should not be distracted by ambiguous source references, confusing language, or incorrect punctuation. It is a good idea to set your draft aside for a day or two, if time allows, so that you can look at it with a fresh eye. It is also a good idea to gather as much feedback as you can from peers. Plan to exchange drafts with a classmate or two for their suggestions (see 1j for more on giving and receiving feedback).

4e   Follow formatting conventions

Research paper formatting conventions are customary ways of presenting information that have developed in various disciplines. Ask your instructor if there is a particular format you should use. If not, select the format from the discipline most closely related to your research topic. Documentation formats for different disciplines are provided in Chapters 6 and 7.

5 Writing in the Disciplines

As a college student, regardless of your major, you are probably taking courses in a number of disciplines—natural and social sciences, humanities and arts, and perhaps even applied courses, such as business, engineering, or consumer economics.

Even though the basic principles of researching and writing in the disciplines share many common elements, such things as the types of questions asked and evidence used, the customary ways in which the information is reported, and the language and writing style preferred often vary from one field of study to another.

Researching and writing, however, are vitally important in all disciplines. This chapter provides a broad overview of disciplinary research and writing.

http://wac.colostate.edu
A site for scholarly exchange about communication across the curriculum, from the WAC Clearinghouse at Colorado State University.

5a Disciplinary research

Broadly defined, all research is systematic inquiry designed to further our knowledge and understanding of a subject. Using this definition, nearly everything you do in college is research. You seek to discover information about people, objects, and nature; to revise your findings in light of new information that comes to your attention; and to interpret your experience and communicate that interpretation to others.

❶ Questions asked in the disciplines

People are interpretive animals. In our interaction with the world, we seek to represent internally to ourselves what we have experienced externally. When we are confronted with a problematic experience, we seek a reasonable explanation for it; that is, we "research" the subject to discover its meaning.

What if an apple fell and hit you on the head? A physicist might ask the following questions: Why does the apple fall? How long will it take to reach the ground? Such questions involve broad issues about the nature of the physical universe and the "laws" that govern it. The physicist observes natural phenomena and then develops a systematic body of principles to account for or predict other similar events in the universe.

A social scientist, perhaps an economist, researching the same issue might focus on the need for a reliable food source in a society, asking such questions as these: How do people meet their basic need for food? What laws of supply and demand operate on the production and distribution of food? An economist also seeks to define the broad issues of how people in society structure their economic relationships. The economist develops a systematic body of ideas to be used in accounting for other similar economic systems or events.

A humanist—perhaps a historian—researching this issue would attempt to explain and explore human experience by asking other questions: What is the significance of the event to those of this particular historical period? How does this event relate to other similar events? The historian would account for, reconstruct, and narrate all the events surrounding the falling apple relating the event to other more general cultural events.

It is clear that researchers in different disciplines ask different questions about the same subject. What distinguishes them is the perspective that the researcher in each field takes.

❷ Evidence used in the disciplines

In addition to asking different questions, researchers in the disciplines have customary ways in which they "prove" their hypotheses or provide reasons for their points of view. For example, evidence to a historian may be a diary or a memoir written during a specific historical period; evidence to a psychologist may be a case study of an individual suffering from a particular mental illness. Anyone who is learning about a specific discipline will also be learning how to argue a case and present evidence in that discipline. Evidence can vary from quantitative (using statistical and numerical data) to qualitative (using observations and interviews). Data can be presented in the form of visuals such as tables, graphics, and charts, or it can be described in narratives (stories). Information can be gathered either through primary sources (first-hand data collection) or through secondary sources (reading and reporting on the work of others).

5b   Disciplinary discourse

In addition to variations in questions and evidence, disciplines can vary in the ways they present information, sometimes called disciplinary genres. Genres are the typical forms that writing and speech can take in various contexts. Your task as an apprentice in a particular discipline is to uncover the discipline's genres and practice them in your own writing.

A discipline's genres will incorporate specific formats in which to organize its writing. The **lab report,** for example, is a genre of scientific writing. A typical lab report will contain the same conventional features and formats for many scientific disciplines. Another genre of both natural and social science writing is the informal research report.

The use of visuals is especially important in fields within the sciences and social sciences. Often data is presented in the form of visuals—tables, graphs, and charts. Such visuals can be very effective, particularly in presenting a great deal of data in a compact form.

Readers of disciplinary genres expect to find certain organizational patterns, certain types of connections between ideas, and a logical sequence. Don't hesitate to ask your instructors for suitable models of what they consider excellent disciplinary writing.

Another distinguishing feature of disciplinary writing is style—the customary sentence patterns chosen by writers in that discipline. Features of style that can differ by disciplines include **tone** (How objective is the writing? How formal is the tone?), **rhetorical stance** (Do the writers try to achieve distance from their audience? Or do they try to identify with their audience?), and **sentence style** (How long are the sentences and paragraphs in this discipline? Are the verbs active or passive? Are headings and subheadings used?).

A third distinguishing feature of disciplinary genres is revealed by their documentation conventions. Even though the general principles of documentation are the same (that is, your goal is to provide your reader with an indication of what sources you used and how to find them), formatting conventions differ by discipline. Documentation styles in various disciplines are discussed in Chapters 6 and 7.

The vocabulary customarily used in a discipline is an important part of its discourse. One of your primary jobs as you study a discipline will be to learn its specialized vocabulary. Not only will you need to recognize the specialized and technical words when you read them, but you will also need to employ these words appropriately in your writing. It may be helpful to keep your own dictionary of specialized terms as you are studying a particular field.

5c   Writing about literature

Readers of literary works ask interpretive or analytical questions: What sort of work is it? Does it have a powerful message? Much of the writing done in college literature courses is interpretive or analytical. Instructors generally expect students to make a claim about a literary work and then support that claim through reasoned arguments and evidence from the work itself and from other scholars. Your goal in writing interpretively or analytically is to shed light on an aspect of the work that the reader might not otherwise see.

WebLink
http://www.crayne.com/howcrit.html
"How to Critique Fiction"—an excellent introduction to literary analysis

❶ Read literature critically

Begin by reading the work critically. Using the following critical reading process when you read a piece of literature will start you on the way to writing an interpretive or analytical essay.

First, read the work straight through, with an eye toward understanding the text and noting how it affects you as a reader. Does the work make you feel happy or sad? Is there a character, event, or scene that is particularly moving or striking? Does anything in the text confuse or puzzle you? Keep a journal in which you jot down impressions as you read.

Once you have finished reading the work, skim it in its entirety to highlight important passages, such as scenes that are pivotal to the plot, revealing character descriptions, and vivid descriptive passages. Then try writing a brief plot outline for the work to be sure that you have a clear sense of the chronology. You might also list key characters and their relationships to each other.

Finally, review your marginal notes, outline, and lists to determine what aspects of the work interested you most. Try freewriting at your computer or in your journal for ten minutes recalling your overall impressions and any important points you may have overlooked earlier.

❷ Determine purpose, persona, and audience

Once you have completed your critical reading, you should establish a rhetorical stance for your paper. Begin by carefully studying the assignment itself.

To decide on your purpose for writing, look for key terms in the assignment, such as *analyze* or *discuss*. Both of these terms imply an interpretive or analytical purpose for writing. Your instructor may have specified some aspect of the work that you should write about, or he or she may have left the topic open-ended. In most cases, your instructor will expect you to write a piece with an argumentative edge that makes a point about the work and supports that point with examples and illustrations from the text.

Next, think about your persona for the paper. How do you wish to come across as a writer? Will you be objective and fair or heated and passionate? Your persona is revealed in the paper through the words and sentence structures you choose.

Finally, ask yourself who the audience for the paper will be. Most often the audience, in addition to your teacher, will be intelligent readers who are interested in literature but who may not be acquainted with the particular work you are writing about. Your paper should provide your readers with background information about the work so that they will be able to follow your argument.

❸ Develop a claim and write a thesis

How you interpret or analyze a work of literature will depend on what you have read, your interests, your prior knowledge, the information presented in class, and your general understanding of the work in question. If you have a choice, you should write about something that interests or intrigues you about the work. You will need to come up with your own critical interpretation or analysis of the work and then write a thesis statement that articulates your claim.

Literary works are typically analyzed with respect to some major aspect such as characters, plot, theme, structure, setting, point of view, rhythm, imagery, symbolism, tone, or voice.

❹ Use the appropriate person and tense

In writing interpretively about literature, it is generally appropriate to use the first person (*I, we, our*) to express your own point of view: "*I* was greatly moved by the character's predicament." However, in academic papers, the third person (*he, she, it, they*) is typically used to discuss information found in sources.

Also, in writing about a work of literature, the commonly accepted practice is to use the present tense (sometimes called the **literary present**) when describing events that happened in the work: "Adam Trask *learns* about his wife's true character slowly." Similarly, use the present tense when discussing what an author has done in a specific literary work: "Steinbeck *uses* Cathy and Adam Trask to illustrate his point about the pure evil that exists in human nature."

5d Writing in the natural and social sciences

The natural sciences hold an authoritative position in society. Using a widely accepted methodology, scientists (including biologists and botanists, mathematicians, physicists and chemists, and geologists and geographers, as well as applied and medical scientists such as pathologists and surgeons, engineers, and computer scientists) formulate and test theories about the natural and physical world, and their findings are used to solve problems in medicine, industry, and agriculture.

The social sciences—psychology, anthropology, political science, sociology, and education—have as their overall goal the systematic, objective study of human behavior and human societies. Social scientists study only the objectively observable aspect of people—behavior. Social scientists write to convey research findings discovered through these observations.

❶ Know the different types of writing in the natural and social sciences

To solve problems in a systematic way, natural scientists use the scientific method. Writing plays a critical role in each step. The first step is to express the problem in writing, clearly and objectively, in the form of a *problem statement*. The second step is to gather all relevant information needed to solve the problem. The third step is to analyze that information and formulate a *hypothesis*—a statement that predicts what the scientist expects to find. The fourth step is to design and conduct controlled experiments to test the hypothesis, keeping detailed records of all the findings. The fifth step is to analyze these records to determine how well they support the hypothesis. Finally, the sixth step is to restate the hypothesis in a conclusion that explains how the experimental data supported, refuted, or modified the initial hypothesis.

Social scientists also use the scientific method much of the time. Writing in the social sciences often begins with the careful recording of field or observation notes, interview transcripts, survey data, or other data collections. From these materials, the social scientist formulates a hypothesis and then seeks to test that hypothesis through further systematic experiments or observations. Notes from this additional data collection are then analyzed and compared to the hypothesis. Finally, as in natural science research, the social scientist writes a conclusion explaining how the experimental or observational data supported, refuted, or modified the initial hypothesis.

Both natural and social scientists typically recount the entire process in a research report. Research reports are based on primary research conducted by scientists. Much natural science research is based on experiments; much social science research is based on surveys, interviews, questionnaires, and observations. It is through primary research that great breakthroughs in the advancement of knowledge are made, and it is through research reports that these developments are announced to the researcher's colleagues, the scientific community, and the world at large. The basic outline for research reports is the same:

- The *abstract* summarizes the report in one compact paragraph.
- The *introduction* states the problem, background information, and hypothesis.
- The *literature review* summarizes related research.
- The section on *research methods* outlines the processes used in the experiments or data-gathering.
- The section on *research results* describes the outcomes and findings.
- The *discussion* and *conclusion* relate the research to the problem and hypothesis and speculate on the implications of the research.
- The *endmatter* includes notes, references, and appendixes.

The second major category of scientific and social science writing is the review of literature. In this type of writing, based on secondary research, the writer discusses the existing literature about the research topic rather than his or her own original research. Only by analyzing and synthesizing the findings of other researchers reported in journal articles and other relevant sources can students and scholars keep up on developments—and controversies—in their fields.

WebLink

http://filebox.vt.edu/eng/mech/writing
An excellent writing workbook for students of science and engineering

❷ Understand your purpose and your audience

When it is used to inform an audience about scientific findings and data, writing in the natural sciences needs to be objective, exact, complete, and correct. In most cases, it describes scientific problems and their solutions.

Much writing in the social sciences is argumentative. You need to take a stand or make a claim about a particular issue and then argue for that position. You can support your argument with primary research or secondary sources (or both).

As a student, when you are writing about the sciences, you are generally responding to an assignment that may specify whether you are to write a research report or a literature review. If it does not, you are probably better off reviewing the literature on a particular topic unless you are already involved in a scientific experiment or data-gathering project. If the assignment calls for primary research, you will probably need your instructor's help in designing an appropriate method for collecting data.

To decide on your purpose for writing, begin by carefully studying the assignment itself. Look for key terms like *analyze* and *discuss*. Both of these terms imply an interpretive or critical purpose for writing. Your instructor will expect you to write a piece that makes a point, supported by secondary sources.

Next, ask yourself who your audience will be. Usually you can assume that you are writing for intelligent readers who are interested in the subject but may not know many details about the topic. You should provide enough background information so that such readers will be able to follow your argument. Because of the focus on objectivity, the writer's personal opinion is not relevant in scientific writing.

To write a thesis in the natural sciences, you need to refine your topic. For example, if you decided to write about life on the space station, you could use print sources and the Internet to find out more about it and then write an informative thesis describing what you found out. If your instructor wanted your report to have an argumentative edge, your thesis could argue for or against the United States's continued participation in the International Space Station.

The thesis of a social science paper will generally relate to a claim about a particular kind of observed behavior. With regard to children and drugs, for example, you might claim (based on a literature review and/or observational or survey data) that parents are the most important determining factor in whether their children experiment with alcohol and drugs.

In any writing assignment, regardless of the discipline, you should follow the writing process described in Chapters 1 through 5 of this handbook. In the sciences, visuals such as graphs, charts, photographs and diagrams are often used to convey information and statistical data in a compact format. As a novice science writer, you will need to learn the customary ways in which statistical data is presented in your field.

6 MLA Documentation

The Modern Language Association (MLA) documentation style has been adopted by many scholarly writers in the fields of language and literature.* The MLA style consists of in-text citations (enclosed in parentheses) and an alphabetical listing of works cited (placed at the end of the paper). For humanities researchers, specific sources and the pages on which information can be found are more important than the date on which the source was published. So in-text citations in the MLA style give the author's last name and the page number of the source information but omit the date.

http://www.mla.org
Click on the "MLA Style" tab for more information

*The *MLA Style Manual and Guide to Scholarly Publishing* (3rd ed., New York: MLA, 2008) makes several significant changes to the MLA's documentation and formatting guidelines. These include italicizing, rather than underlining, all titles; adding both issue and volume number to all journal entries; and adding the medium of publication (Print, Web, Audio, CD, Film, etc.) to every Works Cited entry, as well as a simplified style for online citations. The samples in this handbook reflect the 2008 style.

A Directory to MLA Style

6a   Integrate sources and avoid plagiarism in MLA style

In Chapter 3, "Evaluating and Using Sources: Avoiding Plagiarism," we talked in general about the importance of using sources accurately and responsibly in your research papers. To help you do so, the MLA citation format provides for a two-part system of source identification: (1) parenthetical references within the body of the paper (discussed in 6b), and (2) a Works Cited list at the end of the paper (discussed in 6d). By using MLA style, you can integrate your source information appropriately and ethically without inadvertently committing plagiarism.

MLA Citation Style

1. Introduce your source using a signal phrase that names its author or include the author's last name in parentheses at the end of the citation.

   `According to Jones,... (332) or (Jones 332)`

2. Paraphrase or summarize the information from your source. It's best to use direct quotations sparingly. Recast the source information into your own words. If you do use any words or phrases from the author, however, be sure to put them in quotation marks.

3. At the conclusion of your paraphrase, summary, or quotation, insert in parentheses the page number on which the information was found, followed by a period: (332). or Jones (332).

4. At the end of your paper, list the source with complete bibliographic information on your Works Cited page.

Plagiarism, a serious academic offense, is often inadvertently committed in one of the following ways:

1. Failing to acknowledge a summary or paraphrase of a source in the body of the paper through a signal phrase and parenthetical citation.

2. Using the original authors' words without putting the borrowed words or phrases in quotation marks or including a parenthetical citation.

❶ Acknowledge all sources

A successful research paper is written as an argument in the writer's own words, expressing an understanding of the answers to specific research questions. In such a paper, sources are used as evidence in support of the writer's argument. Source support is integrated into the flow of the research paper through the use of paraphrases and summaries in the writer's own words; each source is acknowledged by a parenthetical citation. Failing to acknowledge a source results in plagiarism. In addition to paraphrases and summaries, any other source material must also be acknowledged, such as specific facts, graphics or visuals, cartoons, diagrams, or charts, using the two-part MLA citation system.

❷ Indicate original source words and phrases with quotation marks

The best research papers use direct quotations sparingly as support for their own ideas and integrate those quotations smoothly into the flow of the paper. A signal phrase alerts the reader that a direct quotation follows; the quotation marks show exactly which words and phrases are being quoted. Long quotations are formatted using indentation rather than quotation marks. Carelessness at the note-taking stage can result in unintentional plagiarism (see 3c).

6b   MLA style for in-text citations

In MLA documentation, citations within the body of the paper are linked to the Works Cited list at the end. The in-text citations are sometimes called **parenthetical references**, because the documentation is placed in parentheses. In MLA style, the author who is being cited and the page number of the source make up the in-text citation.

Following are some guidelines for incorporating parenthetical references in the text of your research paper.

1. Author Named in a Signal Phrase

If a paraphrase or direct quotation is introduced with the name of the author in a signal phrase, simply indicate the page number of the source in parentheses at the end of the cited material.

Attempting to define ethnic stereotyping, Allport states that "much prejudice is a matter of blind conformity with prevailing folkways" (12).

No page number is necessary when an entire work is cited. (Note that titles of independently published works are italicized.)

Conrad's book *Lord Jim* tells the story of an idealistic young Englishman.

2. Author Named in Parentheses

If the author's name is not used to introduce the paraphrased or quoted material, place the author's last name along with the specific page number in parentheses at the end of the cited material. Do not separate author and page number with a comma. Note that the parenthetical material precedes the sentence's end punctuation.

When Mitford and Rodd were first engaged, "they even bought black shirts and went to some Fascist meetings" (Guinness 304).

3. Multiple Sentences Paraphrased

Indicate every instance of paraphrased or summarized material. If an entire paragraph is paraphrased from a single source, mention the author's name at the beginning of the paragraph and cite the page number where appropriate.

As Endelman shows, the turbulence of the interwar years— "political agitation, social discrimination, street hooliganism" (191)—culminated in the formation of the British Union of Fascists. He states that anti-Semitism "was common enough that few Jews could have avoided it altogether or been unaware of its existence" (194).

4. Work by Two or Three Authors

Include the last names of all the authors (the last two connected by *and*) either in the text or in the parenthetical reference. Because the following reference is to the entire work, no page number is necessary.

Goodsell, Maher, and Tinto write about how the theory of
collaborative learning may be applied to the administration of a
college or university.

5. Work by Four or More Authors

In citing a work by four or more authors, either provide the last names of all the authors or provide the name of the first author followed by the abbreviation *et al.* ("and others").

In *The Development of Writing Abilities*, the authors present a theory of
writing based on whether a writer assumes a participant or a spectator
role (Britton et al.).

6. Work by a Corporate Author

When the author is an organization or corporation, treat the group's name the same as the name of an individual author. If the name is long, try to incorporate it into the text rather than including it in a parenthetical note.

The book *Discovering Microsoft Office*, by the Microsoft
Corporation describes "the many multilingual features available
in *Outlook*" (143).

7. Work in More Than One Volume

If the work consists of more than one volume, provide the volume number, followed by a colon, just before the page number.

In Ward's introduction to the collected works of Sir John Vanbrugh, he
states that "the Vanbrugh family seems to have been both ancient and
honorable" (1:x).

When referring to an entire volume of a multivolume work, add a comma after the author's name, followed by *vol.* and the volume number.

8. Different Works by the Same Author

When the Works Cited list refers to two works by the same author, include in the parenthetical reference the title (which may be abbreviated), as well as the author and the page number of the source. If the author's name is included in the text, cite only the title and page number in parentheses.

Her first volume of memoirs, published in 1975, tells the story of her brother's friend (Mitchison, *All Change Here* 85). In her prewar novel, Mitchison, who was the housebound wife of an Oxford don, derives a strange solution to England's economic problems (*We Have Been Warned* 441).

9. Works by Two or More Authors with the Same Last Name

Include both the authors' first and last names in the signal phrase or in parentheses to distinguish two authors who have the same last name.

Luci Shaw reveals deep spirituality in her poem titled "Made Flesh" (31). Martin Shaw's poem "Respite" is more philosophical (45).

10. Work Cited Indirectly

If possible, take information directly from the original source. However, sometimes it is necessary to cite someone indirectly—particularly in the case of a published account of someone's spoken words. To indicate an indirect quotation, use the abbreviation *qtd. in* (for "quoted in") before listing the source.

High school teacher Ruth Gerrard finds that "certain Shakespearean characters have definite potential as student role models" (qtd. in Davis and Salomone 24).

11. Two or More Sources Within the Same Citation

When referring to two or more sources within the same parenthetical reference, use semicolons to separate the citations. For the sake of readability, however, take care not to list too many sources in a single citation.

The works of several authors in the postwar years tend to focus on racial themes (Mitchison 440; Mosley 198).

12. Anonymous Work

Sources such as magazine articles, Web sites, and reports by commissions may not list an author. Such works are listed by their titles on the Works Cited page. For the in-text citation of an anonymous work listed by title, use an abbreviated version of the title, in parentheses.

The article points out the miscommunications that can occur between men and women because of differences in communication styles ("It Started" 110).

13. Work of Literature

Classic works of literature are often available in different editions. It is therefore helpful to include location information, such as chapter number, section number, or act and scene number, in the parenthetical reference so that the reader can locate the reference in any edition of the work. Include this location information after a page reference, where appropriate. When citing classic poetry or plays, use the line numbers instead of page numbers. Generally, use arabic numbers rather than roman numerals.

In the novel *Lord Jim*, Conrad describes the village of Patusan and its inhabitants (242; ch. 24).

In *Paradise Lost*, Satan's descent to earth is described in graphic detail (Milton 4.9-31).

As Laertes leaves for France, Polonius gives the young man trite and unhelpful advice such as "Beware / Of entrance to a quarrel; but being in, / Bear't that th' opposed may beware of thee" (*Hamlet* 1.3.65-67).

14. Work in an Anthology

If you are citing a work found in an anthology (collection), use the name of the author of the particular work you are citing, not the editors of the anthology. List the page numbers as they are found in the anthology.

```
The American dream crosses many ethnic boundaries, as illustrated by

Papaleo (88).
```

15. Sacred Text

When quoting from the Bible, give the title of the version (e.g., *Revised Standard Version*), the book of the Bible, the chapter and verse (separated by a period). If using a signal phrase, spell out the book of the Bible being quoted. In parentheses, abbreviate the book of the Bible if its name is five or more letters (e.g., Phil. for Philippians). Give the same types of details for the Qur'an or other sacred works.

```
In his letter to the Philippians, the apostle Paul says, "There must be

no room for rivalry and personal vanity among you, but you must humbly

reckon others better than yourselves. Look to each other's interest and

not merely to your own" (The New English Bible, Phil. 2.3-4).
```

16. Entire Work or One-Page Article

When citing an entire work or a work that is only one page long, refer to the text in a signal phrase by the author and title without any page numbers.

```
In his book Losing My Mind: An Intimate Look at Life with Alzheimer's,

Thomas DeBaggio chronicles his battle with Alzheimer's disease.
```

17. Work with No Page Numbers

If you are citing a work that does not have any page numbers listed, you may omit the page number from your citation. If a work uses paragraph numbers instead of page numbers, use the abbreviation *par.* or *pars.*

```
The reporter from a recent Family Law Conference sponsored by the American

Bar Association, Sarah H. Ramsey, stated, "High-conflict custody cases are
```

marked by a lack of trust between the parents, a high level of anger, and
a willingness to engage in repetitive litigation" (par. 24).

18. Electronic or Online Source

When information is from an electronic medium, often the entire work is referenced. In such cases, incorporate the reference to the work within the sentence by naming the author of the source (or the title, if no author is listed) just as it is listed on the Works Cited page.

One of the features of *The Encyclopedia Mythica* Web site is its
archive of cultural myths, such as those prevalent in Native American
society.

19. Secondary Web Page Source

When citing a Web site with secondary pages, list separately each secondary page used in the research paper.

According to *Britannica Online*, in Native American mythology, a feather
often symbolizes a prayer ("Feather").

20. Quotation or Paraphrase from an Electronic Source

When quoting or paraphrasing directly from an electronic source, either give the section title in quotation marks (as in item 19) or cite the paragraph number (with the abbreviation *par.*), if provided, so that a reader will be able to find the section used in the paper. If no numbering is provided, list the source author or title only.

The writer discusses his reasons for calling Xerox's online site "a great
place to visit" (Gomes, par. 5).

The average global air temperature has risen between 0.3 and 0.6 degrees
Celsius (Hileman).

6c   MLA style for bibliographic footnotes and endnotes

Generally, footnotes and endnotes are not used in MLA style of documentation. However, notes may be included to refer the reader to sources that contain information different from the content of the paper. In the text, indicate a note with a superscript number typed immediately after the source that is referred to. Number notes consecutively throughout the text.

Use a note to cite sources that have additional information on topics covered in the paper.

[1] For further information on this point, see Barbera (168), McBrien (56), and Kristeva (29).

Use a note to cite sources that contain information related to that included in the paper.

[2] Although outside the scope of this paper, major themes in the novel are discussed by Kristeva and Barbera.

Use a note to cite sources containing information that a reader might want to compare with that in the paper.

[3] On this point, see also Rosenblatt's *Literature as Exploration*, in which she discusses reader response theory.

For the endnote format, start a new page following the end of the text, before the Works Cited list. Type the title "Notes," centered horizontally one inch from the top of the page. Double-space to the first note. Indent the first line five spaces (or one-half inch) from the left margin, and type the note number slightly above the line (or use the superscript format on a word processor). Follow this number with one space and then the text of the note. Double-space between and within all notes.

For the footnote format, position the text of the note at the bottom of the page on which the reference occurs. Begin the footnote four lines below the text. Single-space within a footnote, but double-space between footnotes if more than one note appears on a page. On the Works Cited page, include all the sources mentioned in the notes.

6d MLA style for the Works Cited page

The alphabetical listing of all the sources used in a paper, usually titled Works Cited, comes at the end of the paper. Other names for this listing include Bibliography, Literature Cited, Works Consulted (which includes works not directly cited), and Annotated Bibliography (which includes brief summaries of sources). Check with your instructor to determine which format to use. The purpose of this listing is to help readers find the information used in the paper, so the entries must be complete and accurate.

List sources alphabetically by the last name of the author, using the letter-by-letter system of alphabetization. When no author is given, alphabetize by the first word of the title (excluding *A, An*, or *The*). Type the first word of each entry at the left margin. Indent subsequent lines of the same entry five spaces (or one-half inch). Double-space the entire reference page, both between and within entries.

When you have more than one work by the same author, arrange the titles alphabetically. Give the author's name for the first entry only. For subsequent works by the same author, substitute three hyphens (followed by a period) for the author's name.

Books   A citation for a book has four basic parts:

Author's Name. *Book Title*. Publication Information. Medium.

For books, monographs, and other complete works, include the author's full name as given on the title page—start with the last name first, followed by a comma; then put the first name and middle name or initial followed by a period. After the author's name, give the complete title of the work as it appears on the title page (italicized), followed by a period. Important words in the title should be capitalized. Include the subtitle, if there is one, separated from the title by a colon. Next, include (if appropriate) the name of the editor, compiler, or translator; the edition of the book; the number of volumes; and the name of the series. Finally, indicate the place of publication, followed by a colon (if several cities are listed, include only the first one); the publisher's name as it appears on the title page, followed by a comma; and the date of publication from the copyright page, followed by a period. Finally, include the medium of publication, such as print.

In MLA style, the publication information is abbreviated as much as is possible in the bibliographic entry. The city where the book was published is given without a state abbreviation. A country abbreviation may be needed for clarity for some foreign publications (for example, *Ulster, Ire.; Bergen, Norw.*). But if a foreign city is well known (such as London or Paris), a country abbreviation is unnecessary. Shorten the publisher's name to one word wherever possible (for example, McGraw-Hill, Inc., to *McGraw*; Houghton Mifflin Co. to *Houghton*). Similarly, abbreviate the names of university and government presses: *Columbia UP* stands for Columbia University Press; the letters *GPO* for Government Printing Office. (For guidelines on citing electronic books, see items 52 and 53.)

1. Book by One Author

Author's Name   Book Title   Publication Information

Bryant, John. *The Fluid Text*. Ann Arbor: U of Michigan P, 2002. Print.

Haire-Sargeant, Lin. *H*. New York: Pocket, 1992. Print.

Manguel, Alberto. *A History of Reading*. New York: Viking, 1996. Print.

2. Book by Two or Three Authors

Write multiple authors' names in the order in which they are given on the book's title page. Note that this order may not be alphabetical. Reverse the name of the first author only, putting the last name first; separate the authors' names with commas.

Fiorina, Morris P., Sammuel J. Abrams, and Jeremy C, Pope. *Culture War?*

    The Myth of a Polarized America. New York: Longman, 2005. Print.

3. Book by More Than Three Authors

For a book with more than three authors, either write out the names of all the authors listed on the book's title page or write only the first author's name, followed by a comma and the Latin phrase *et al.* (for "and others").

Britton, James, Tony Burgess, Nancy Martin, Alex McLeod, and Harold

   Rosen. *The Development of Writing Abilities*. London: Macmillan,

   1975. Print.

Britton, James, et al. *The Development of Writing Abilities*. London:

   Macmillan, 1975. Print.

4. Organization as Author

When an organization rather than an individual is the author, give the name of the organization as listed on the title page instead of the author, even if the same group also published the book.

Alzheimer's Disease and Related Disorders Association. *Understanding*

   Alzheimer's Disease. New York: Scribner's, 1988. Print.

5. Book by a Corporate Author

A book by a corporate author is any book whose title page lists a group as the author rather than individuals. Start with the name of the corporate author, even if it is also the publisher.

Conference on College Composition and Communication. *The National*

   Language Policy. Urbana: NCTE, 1992. Print.

6. Unknown Author

If no author is listed, begin the entry with the title. List the work on your references, listing alphabetically by the first word in the title (ignoring *A, An,* or *The*) instead of by the author.

The American Heritage Dictionary of the English Language. 4th ed. Boston:

   Houghton, 2002. Print.

7. Book with an Editor

For books with editors rather than authors, start with the editor or editors, followed by a comma and *ed.* (for "editor") or *eds.* (for "editors").

Barbera, Jack, and William McBrien, eds. *Me Again: The Uncollected*

    Writings of Stevie Smith. New York: Farrar, 1982. Print.

8. Chapter or Selection from an Edited Work

An entry for a particular selection needs to begin with the author's name and the title of the selection. The title is italicized if the work is a book or a play; it is enclosed in quotation marks if the work is a poem, short story, chapter, or essay. Note that the name of the editor or editors follows the book title and is preceded by the abbreviation *Ed.* (for "Edited by"). The inclusive page numbers of the work follow the publication information. The publication medium is last.

Rushdie, Salman. "Chekov and Zulu." *The Longman Anthology of British*

    Literature: The Twentieth Century. Ed. David Damrosch, Kevin J. H.

    Dettmar, and Jennifer Wicke. 3rd ed. New York: Longman, 2006.

    2989-98. Print.

9. Book with Author and Editor

When citing the book itself, begin with the author's name. The editor's name, introduced by *Ed.*, follows the title.

L'Engle, Madeleine. *O Sapientia*. Ed. Luci Shaw. Wheaton: Shaw, 1984.

    Print.

When citing the editor's contribution to the work, begin with the editor's name followed by a comma and *ed.* Then list the author's name, introduced by *By*, following the title.

Shaw, Luci, ed. *O Sapientia*. By Madeleine L'Engle. Wheaton: Shaw, 1984.

    Print.

10. Two or More Items from an Anthology

When citing more than one work from an anthology, list the anthology itself in your Works Cited.

```
Madison, Soyini D., ed. The Woman That I Am: The Literature and Culture
    of Contemporary Women of Color. New York: St. Martin's, 1994. Print.
```

11. Two or More Books by the Same Author

Alphabetize entries by the first word in the title. Include the author's name in the first entry only. In subsequent entries, type three hyphens in place of the author's name, followed by a period.

```
Rose, Mike. Lives on the Boundary: A Moving Account of the Struggles and
    Achievements of America's Educationally Underprepared. New York:
    Penguin, 1989. Print.
---. Possible Lives: The Promise of Education in America. Boston:
    Houghton, 1995. Print.
```

12. Article in a Reference Book

An entry for an article in a reference book follows the same pattern as an entry for a work in an anthology. Note, however, that the editor's name and full publication information need not be provided; it is sufficient to provide the edition (if known) and the year of publication. If the article is signed, provide the author's name. (Often the author's name is given in abbreviated form at the end of the article and included in full form elsewhere.)

```
Robins, Robert Henry. "Language." Encyclopaedia Britannica. 2007 ed.
    Print.
```

If the article is unsigned, start with the title of the article:

```
"Lochinvar." Merriam-Webster's Encyclopedia of Literature. 1995 ed.
    Print.
```

13. Introduction, Preface, Foreword, or Afterword

Start with the name of the author of the specific part being cited, followed by the name of the part, capitalized but not underlined or enclosed in quotation marks. If the writer of the part is the same as the author of the book, give the author's last name, preceded by the word *By*. If the writer of the part is different from the author of the book, give the book author's complete name after *By*. Provide complete publication information and inclusive page numbers (even if they are given as Roman numerals) of the part being cited.

```
Tompkins, Jane. Preface. A Life in School: What the Teacher Learned. By

    Tompkins. Reading: Addison, 1996. xi-xix. Print.
```

14. Book in Translation

Begin the entry with the author's name and the title of the book. After the book's title, insert the abbreviation *Trans.* (for "Translated by") and give the translator's name. If the book also has an editor, give the names of the editor and the translator in the order in which they are listed on the title page.

```
Kristeva, Julia. Powers of Horror: An Essay on Abjection. Trans. Leon S.

    Roudiez. New York: Columbia UP, 1982. Print.
```

15. Second or Subsequent Edition of a Book

If a book is not a first edition, list the edition the way it is identified on the book's title page: by year (*1993 ed.*), by name (*Rev. ed.* for "Revised edition"), or by number (*2nd ed., 3rd ed.*).

```
Strunk, William, Jr., E. B. White, and Roger Angell. The Elements of

    Style. 4th ed. New York: Longman, 2000. Print.
```

16. Work in More Than One Volume

When citing more than one volume of a multivolume work, insert the total number of volumes in the work before the publication material.

```
Doyle, Arthur Conan. The Complete Sherlock Holmes. 2 vols. Garden City:

    Doubleday, 1930. Print.
```

17. One Volume of a Multivolume Work

Provide the author and title followed by the volume number of the volume you are citing. At the end of the citation, following the date, provide the number of volumes in the complete work.

```
Poe, Edgar Allan. The Complete Poems and Stories of Edgar Allan Poe. Vol.

    1. New York: Knopf, 1982. 2 vols. Print.
```

18. Book in a Series

If the title page indicates that the book is part of a series, insert the series name (do not italicize it or enclose it in quotation marks) and the series number, if any, before the publication information.

```
Ball, Arnetha F., and Ted Lardner. African American Literacies Unleashed:

    Vernacular English and the Composition Classroom. Studies in Writing

    and Rhetoric. Urbana: NCTE, 2005. Print.
```

19. Republished Book

Insert the original publication date, followed by a period, before the publication material of the work being cited.

```
Dewey, John. Experience and Education. 1938. New York: Collier, 1963.

    Print.
```

20. Government Document

If the author of a government document is unknown, start with the name of the government, followed by the name of the agency that issued the document, abbreviated. The title of the publication, underlined, follows, and the usual publication material completes the entry.

```
United States. FBI. Uniform Crime Reports for the United States: 1995.

    Washington: GPO, 1995. Print.
```

(*GPO* stands for Government Printing Office.)

21. Published Proceedings of a Conference

Write an entry for proceedings in the same way as for a book. Provide information about the conference after the title of the proceedings.

```
Chambers, Jack A., ed. College Teaching and Learning. Selected Papers

    from the 13th Intl. Conf. on Coll. Teaching and Learning, Apr. 2002.

    Jacksonville: Florida Community Coll. at Jacksonville, 2002. Print.
```

22. Pamphlet or Newsletter

Cite a pamphlet the same way that you would cite a book.

Five Wishes. Aging with Dignity Pamphlet. Princeton: Robert Wood Johnson

    Foundation, 2008. Print.

23. Title Within Another Title

If there is a title of another book within the title of the book you are citing, do not italicize that title within another title.

Steinbeck, John. *Journal of a Novel*: *The* East of Eden *Letters*. New York:

    Viking, 1969. Print.

24. Sacred Text

When citing an individual published edition of a sacred book, begin the entry with the title, including the specific version.

The Torah: The Five Books of Moses. Philadelphia: Jewish Society of

    America, 1962. Print.

Periodicals   A citation for an article in a periodical (journal, magazine, or newspaper) follows a format similar to that for a book:

Author's Name. "Title of the Article." Publication Information. Medium.

In the publication information, the title of the journal, as it appears on the journal's title page (without introductory articles such as *A* and *The*), is italicized. The volume and issue numbers of the publication go after the journal title and are followed by the publication date, in parentheses. A colon follows the parentheses. Then inclusive page numbers are provided for the entire article. Finally, include the publication medium, such as print.

When citing magazines and newspapers, list the day and month (abbreviated except for May, June, and July) of publication, with the day before the month, followed by the year (5 Jan. 2006). Provide page numbers for the entire article. Note that if the article is not printed on consecutive pages, you need to provide only the first page number and a plus sign, with no space between them. (For guidelines on citing articles in online periodicals, see items 56–63.)

25. Article in a Journal Paginated by Volume

For all scholarly journals, include both the volume and issue number. This represents a change from prior MLA style. The issue is indicated by placing a period after the volume number, followed by the issue number—for example, *12.1* signifies volume 12, issue 1, regardless of pagination.

```
        Author                  Article Title
┌──────────────────┐  ┌──────────────────────┐
Cooper, Marilyn M. "Bringing Forth Worlds."

     Computers and Composition 22.1 (2005): 31-38.  Print.
     └──────────────────────┘ └──┘ └─────┘ └────┘  └────┘
          Journal Title        Volume/  Year of  Consecutive  Medium
                               Number  Publication  Pages
```

When there are two or more authors, write the authors' names in the order in which they are given on the first page of the article. This may not be alphabetical. Reverse the name of the first author only (putting the last name first).

Kidda, Michael, Joseph Turner, and Frank E. Parker. "There Is an

     Alternative to Remedial Education." *Metropolitan Universities* 3.3

     (1993): 16-25. Print.

26. Article in a Journal Paginated by Issue

Include both volume and issue numbers regardless of pagination by volume or issue.

Mohanty, S. P. "Us and Them: On the Philosophical Bases of

     Political Criticism." *Yale Journal of Criticism* 2.2 (1989):

     1-31. Print.

27. Magazine Article

If the article is unsigned, begin with the title. For a weekly or biweekly magazine, provide the day, the month (abbreviated, except for May, June, and July), and the year, followed by a colon and the inclusive page numbers.

"It Started in a Garden." *Time* 22 Sept. 1952: 110-11. Print.

For a monthly or quarterly magazine, give only the month or quarter and the year before the inclusive page numbers. (If the article is not printed on consecutive pages, give the first page number followed by a plus sign.)

MacDonald, Heather. "Downward Mobility: The Failure of Open Admissions at

City University." *City Journal* Summer 1994: 10-20. Print.

28. Newspaper Article

Provide the name of the newspaper in italics but do not use the article (*The, An, A*) that precedes it (*Boston Globe*, not *The Boston Globe*). If it is not included in the newspaper's title, add the city of publication in brackets following the title. Nationally published newspapers, such as *USA Today*, do not need a city of publication in the reference. Next, provide the day, month (abbreviated, except for May, June, and July), and year. (Do not list volume or issue numbers; however, if the edition is given on the newspaper's masthead, do include it, followed by a colon.) Conclude the entry with the page numbers, preceded by the section number or letter if each section is separately paginated.

Rose, Maria Matzer. "Jet Blue Bound for Port Columbus." *Columbus Dispatch*

13 July 2006: B1+. Print.

"Twenty Percent Biased Against Jews." *New York Times* 22 Nov. 1992: A1.

Print.

29. Editorial

Provide the name of the editorial writer (last name first), if known, and then the title of the editorial (in quotation marks). Next, write the word *Editorial*, but do not underline it or enclose it in quotation marks. End the entry with the name of the newspaper, magazine, or journal and the standard publication information.

Warner, Judith. "What Girls Ought to Learn from Boys:

Crisis." Editorial. *New York Times* 12 July 2006: A22.

Print.

30. Letter to the Editor

Include the designation *Letter* after the name of the letter writer, but do not underline it or use quotation marks. End the entry with the name of the newspaper, magazine, or journal and the standard publication information.

Lopez, Francisca. Letter. *New York Times* 12 July 2006: A21. Print.

31. Review

Start with the name of the reviewer and the title of the review. Then insert *Rev. of* (for "Review of"), but do not italicize it or enclose it in quotation marks. Next, provide the title of the piece reviewed, followed by a comma, the word *by*, and the name of the author of the piece being reviewed. If the name of the reviewer is not given, start with the title of the review; if no title is given either, start with *Rev. of*. End the entry with the name of the newspaper, magazine, or journal and the standard publication information and medium.

Denby, David. "Dressed to Kill." Rev. of *The Devil Wears Prada. New*

    Yorker 10 July 2006: 119-20. Print.

32. Abstract from an Abstracts Journal

Begin by providing publication information on the original work. Then provide material on the journal in which you found the abstract: the title (italicized), the volume and issue number, and the year (in parentheses), followed by a colon and the page or item number.

Johnson, Nancy Kay. "Cultural and Psychosocial Determinants of Health and

    Illness." Diss. U of Washington, 1980. *DAI* 40 (1980): 425B. Print.

(*Diss.* means "Dissertation," and *DAI* is the abbreviation for *Dissertation Abstracts International*.)

Juliebo, Moira, et al. "Metacognition of Young Readers in an Early

    Intervention Reading Programme." *Journal of Research in Reading* 21.1

    (1998): 24-35. *Psychological Abstracts* 85.7 (1998): item 22380.

    Print.

33. Unsigned Article

If an article has no known author, begin with its title, alphabetizing the citation by the first major word of the title on your references list.

"What You Don't Know about Desktops Can Cost You." *Consumer Reports* Sept.

2002: 20-22. Print.

Other Sources

34. Film or Video Recording

Begin with the film's title (italicized), followed by the director, distributor, and year of release; also provide other pertinent material, such as the names of the performers, writers, and producers, between the title and the name of the distributor. End with the medium.

The Devil Wears Prada. Dir. David Frankel. Perf. Meryl Streep and Anne

Hathaway. 20th Century Fox, 2006. Film.

35. Television or Radio Program

Provide the title of the episode (enclosed in quotation marks), if known; the title of the program (italicized); the title of the series (not italicized or enclosed in quotation marks), if any; the network; the call numbers or letters and local city, if any; and the date of broadcast.

"Bingo to You, Sir." *All Things Considered.* Natl. Public Radio, WBUR,

Boston. 29 Aug. 2006. Radio.

"Ultimate Bear." *National Geographic World Premier.* National Geographic

Channel. 30 Aug. 2006. Television.

36. Sound Recording

For a sound recording that is available commercially, provide the name of the artist, the title of the recording (italicized, unless the piece is identified only by form, number, and key), the manufacturer, and the year of issue. Indicate the medium last.

```
Ormandy, Eugene, cond. Symphony no. 3 in C minor, op. 78. By Camille

      Saint-Saens. Perf. E. Power Biggs, organ. Philadelphia Orch. Sony,

      1991. CD.

Ashanti, "Still on It." Collectibles by Ashanti. Def Jam, 2005. CD.
```

37. Performance

An entry for a play, concert, opera, or dance begins with the title (italicized), includes information similar to that given for a film, and ends with the performance site (for example, the theater and city) and the date of the performance and the medium.

```
Blues for an Alabama Sky. By Pearl Cleage. Dir. Kenny Leon. Perf.

      Phylicia Rashad, Tyrone Mitchell Henderson, Sean C. Squire, Deidre

      N. Henry, and John Henry Redwood. Huntington Theatre, Boston. 5 Feb.

      1997. Performance.
```

38. Work of Art

Provide the name of the artist, the title of the work (italicized), the name of the site that houses the work, and the city. If it is available, include the date the work was created immediately after the title. If the work is part of a private collection, provide the collector's name. When the source is the original work of art, include the medium of composition after the date of composition. When the source is a reproduction, include the medium at the end (*Web*), followed by the date of access.

```
Cassatt, Mary. Breakfast in Bed. 1886. Oil on Canvas. Private collection

      of Dr. and Mrs. John J. McDonough, Youngstown, OH.

---. Five o'Clock Tea. Museum of Fine Arts, Boston. Web. 19 June 2008.
```

39. Published Interview

Provide the name of the person being interviewed; the title of the interview (enclosed in quotation marks), if any; the title of the source in which the interview is published; and any other pertinent bibliographic material, including the medium.

Faulkner, William. "The Meaning of 'A Rose for Emily.'" Interview. 1959.

    The Story and Its Writer: An Introduction to Short Fiction. Ed. Ann

    Charters. Compact 4th ed. Boston: Bedford, 1995. 772-73. Print.

40. Unpublished Interview

Provide the name of the person being interviewed, the designation *Personal interview* (neither italicized nor in quotation marks), and the date of the interview.

Jensen, Steven. Personal interview. 12 Apr. 1997.

41. Personal Letter to the Author

Gore, Al. Letter to the author. 12 Dec. 2005.

42. Dissertation—Published

Cite a published dissertation as a book, but add dissertation information before the publication data. Enclose the title of the dissertation in quotation marks, followed by the abbreviation *Diss.* (for "Dissertation"), the name of the degree-granting institution, a comma, and the year written.

Deatherage, Cynthia. *A Way of Seeing: The Anglo-Saxons and the Primal World*

    View. Diss. Purdue U, 1997. Ann Arbor: UMI, 1997. 9821728. Print.

UMI stands for University Microfilms International. (For an example of a dissertation abstract citation, see item 32.)

43. Dissertation—Unpublished

Balkema, Sandra. "The Composing Activities of Computer-Literate Writers."

    Diss. U of Michigan, 1984. Print.

44. Speech or Lecture

Provide the name of the speaker; the title of the presentation (in quotation marks), if known; the meeting and sponsoring organization, if applicable; the place where the speech or lecture was given; and the date.

Wiesel, Elie. "Night." Opening Banquet. NCTE Convention. Gaylord Opryland

    Hotel and Conference Center, Nashville. 16 Nov. 2006. Speech.

45. Map or Chart

Cite a map or a chart the same way you would cite a book with an unknown author, but add the label *Map* or *Chart* to distinguish it.

```
Wyoming. Map. Chicago: Rand, 1990. Print.
```

46. Cartoon or Comic Strip

```
Schultz, Charles. "Peanuts." Cartoon. Herald Journal [Logan] 15 Aug.

    2002: C6. Print.
```

47. Advertisement

First name the item being advertised; then add the word *Advertisement* and supply the rest of the citation, indicating the source where the ad appeared.

```
Benadryl Severe Allergy and Sinus Headache. Advertisement. Prevention

    Sept. 2002: 55. Print.
```

Electronic Media   The updated 2008 MLA style for electronic sources has been simplified to provide only the information needed to retrieve the document. A URL is typically not required, unless your reader will be unable to locate the source without it. If needed, place the URL in angle brackets after the date of access. End the citation with a period after the angle brackets, as in item 83.

WebLink   http://www.mla.org
MLA's Web site includes
information about citing
electronic media

48. Entire Internet Site

Many times it is appropriate to reference an entire Internet Web site, such as a scholarly project or an information database. Include the information available at the site, in the following sequence:

1. The title of the site or project (italicized)
2. The creator or editor of the site (if given and relevant)

3. The electronic publication information: version number (if relevant), date of electronic publication or latest update, the name of the sponsoring organization or institution (if provided)
4. The medium and the date of access

Pew Center on Global Climate Change: Working Together. 2006. Pew Center

on Global Climate Change. Web. 15 June 2006.

MSN.com. 2003. Microsoft Network. Web. 28 Feb. 2003.

To cite an anonymous article from a reference database, start with the title of the article (in quotation marks). Continue with the electronic publication information from the reference work.

"Feather." *Britannica Online*. Vers. 98.1.1. May 1998. Encyclopaedia

Britannica. Web. 12 Aug. 1998.

49. Course Homepage

If you wish to cite a course homepage, first list the name of the instructor (last name first), then the title of the course (neither italicized nor in quotation marks). Next comes a description, like *Course homepage* (again, neither italicized nor in quotation marks), the dates of the course, the names of the department and institution that offered the course, the medium, and the date of access. [*Note*: MLA spells *home page* as two words.]

Edwards, Farrell. General Physics. Course home page. Jan. 2003-May 2003.

Physics Dept. Utah State U. Web. 6 May 2003.

50. Academic Department's Homepage

Begin a citation for a department with its name, then a description, such as *Dept. home page* (neither italicized nor in quotation marks), the institution's name, the date it was last updated (if provided), the medium, and the date of access.

Department of English. Dept. home page. Utah State U. Web. 16 June 2003.

51. Personal Homepage

When citing someone's homepage, begin with that person's name, followed by the title of the site or, if none is provided, with the description *Home page* (neither italicized nor in quotation marks). Next, provide the date the site was last updated (if provided), the medium, and the date of access.

```
Avila, Alejandro Perez. Home page. 17 Feb. 2003. Web. 1 May 2003.
```

52. Online Book

The complete texts of many books are now available online through databases or scholarly projects, as well as in print. Provide the following items when citing such works:

1. The name of the author (if only an editor, compiler, or translator is mentioned, give that person's name first, followed by *ed., comp.,* or *trans).*
2. The title of the work, italicized
3. The name of any editor, compiler, or translator (if not given earlier)
4. Publication information from the printed work if the work has been printed
5. The name of the sponsoring database or scholarly project
6. The medium and access date

```
Woolf, Virginia. The Voyage Out. London: Faber, 1914. The EServer. Ed.

     Geoffrey Sauer. 2003. U of Washington. Web. 1 June 2003.
```

53. Part of an Online Book

Sometimes you will be referring to a part of an online book. In such a case, list the title of the part after the author's name. If the part is a work like a poem or an essay, use quotation marks. If the part is a customary section like an introduction or a preface, do not include quotation marks. Be sure to give the complete URL of the specific part of the book if it is different from the entire book's URL.

```
Pope, Alexander. "Epistle I." Essay on Man. The EServer. Ed. Geoffrey

     Sauer. 2003. U of Washington. Web. 1 June 2003.
```

54. Online Government Document

When citing government documents, start first with the information from the printed version and conclude with the electronic citation information.

United States. Dept. of Commerce. U.S. Census Bureau. *How the Census*

Bureau Measures Poverty. 26 Aug. 2004. Web. 5 May 2006.

55. Article in an Online Periodical

Many magazines, newspapers, and scholarly journals are now available online. Generally, citations for online periodicals follow the same sequence as citations for print periodicals. They should include the following:

1. The author's name, if provided
2. The title of the work, in quotation marks
3. The name of the journal, magazine, or newspaper, italicized (omit introductory *A* or *The*)
4. The volume and issue number (or other identifying number if provided)
5. The date of publication
6. The range or total number of pages, paragraphs, or sections, if they are numbered
7. The medium and date of access

56. Article in an Online Scholarly Journal via a Journal Database

In addition to scholarly journals that are published online independently (see item 55), others can be accessed via an online journal database. To list such an article, provide the name of the database (italicized) following the print information; end with the medium and your access date. If page numbers are not included, use *n. pag.*

Rosenthal, Angela. "Raising Hair." *Eighteenth-Century Studies* 38.1

(2004): 1-16. *Project Muse.* Web. 14 May 2006.

57. Article in an Online Newspaper or on a Newswire

Stout, David. "Bush Asserts Shield Could've Blocked Missile." *New York*

Times. New York Times, 7 July 2006. Web. 20 July 2006.

58. Article in an Online Magazine

Citron, Roger. "Process Makes Perfect: John Roberts' Marked, and
    Positive, Influence on the Supreme Court." *Slate*. Slate, 7 July
    2006. Web. 20 July 2006.

59. Online Review

Bast, Joseph L. Rev. of *Our Stolen Future*, by Theo Colborn
    et al. *Heartland Institute* 18 Apr. 1996: 27 pars. Web.
    25 June 2006.

60. Online Abstract

Reid, Joy. "Responding to ESL Students' Texts." *TESOL Quarterly*
    28.2 (1994): 273-92. Abstract. Web. 12 July 2006.

61. Anonymous Article

"London Marks 1-Year Anniversary of Carnage." *MSNBC*. MSNBC, 7 July 2006.
    Web. 12 July 2006.

62. Online Editorial

"A Nuclear Threat from India." Editorial. *New York Times*. New York Times,
    13 May 1998. Web. 14 May 2005.

63. Online Letter to the Editor

Lowry, Heath. Letter. *Deseret News Online*. Deseret News, 23 Mar. 1998.
    Web. 25 Mar. 1998.

64. Information Database or Scholarly Project

CNN Interactive. Cable News Network, 12 July 2000. Web. 12 July 2000.

The Electronic Text Center. Ed. David Seaman. 2002. Web. 1 Jan.

   2003.

65. Document from an Information Database

   To cite a poem, short story, article, or other work within a database, begin with the author's name, if given, followed by the title of the work in quotation marks. If no author's name is given, begin with the title. Continue with relevant information on the project, including the medium and the access date.

Angelou, Maya. "On the Pulse of Morning." *Electronic Text Center.*

   Ed. David Seaman. 2002. Web. 1 Jan. 2003.

66. Work from a Personal Subscription Service

   If you are using a personal subscription service, such as AOL, that allows you to locate documents by using keywords, provide the name of the online service (italicized) and the date of access, followed by the keyword.

"Demand for Organic Food Outstrips Supply." *AOL News.* America Online,

   7 July 2006. Web. 7 July 2006. Keyword: Health.

67. Work from a Library Subscription Service

   To cite online documents or articles that you derive from a service that your library subscribes to (e.g., *Lexis-Nexis*), follow the citation for the source itself with the name of the service (italicized), and the date of access. If the service only provides a starting page for the article's original printed version rather than numbering the pages, provide the number followed by a hyphen, a space, and a period: "115- ."

King, Marsha. "Companies Here Ponder Scout Ruling." *Seattle Times* 6 July

   2000: A1. *Lexis-Nexis.* Web. 15 Aug. 2000.

Bozell, Brent L., III. "Fox Hits Bottom--or Does It?" *Human Events*

　　57.4 (2001):15-. *Academic Search Premier*. EBSCO. Web.

　　15 Oct. 2002.

68. Nonperiodical Publication on CD-ROM or Disc

Often works on electronic media are published in a single edition, much as books are. To cite such publications, use a format similar to that used to cite print books, with the addition of the publication medium.

National Geographic Maps. Washington: Natl. Geographic Soc., 2006. CD.

69. Database Periodically Published on CD-ROM

When citing periodically published reference works, include the information on the printed source, the publication medium, the name of the vendor (if relevant), and the electronic publication date.

Arms, Valerie M. "A Dyslexic Can Compose on a Computer." *Educational*

　　Technology 24.1 (1984): 39-41. *ERIC*. Sept. 1990. CD.

70. Multidisc Publication

To cite a CD-ROM publication on multiple discs, list the number of discs or the specific number of the disc you used.

Great Literature Plus. 4 discs. Parsippany: Bureau of Electronic

　　Publishing, 1993. CD.

71. Work in More Than One Medium

When a work is published in more than one medium (for example, both as a book and as a CD or both as a CD and as a disc), you may specify all the media or only the medium you used.

Hult, Christine A., and Thomas N. Huckin. *The New Century Handbook*.

　　4th ed. New York: Longman, 2008. Print, CD.

72. Work in an Indeterminate Electronic Medium

If you cannot tell what medium the source is in (perhaps you accessed the work from a library's Web site and are unsure whether it is on CD-ROM or stored on the library's Internet server), use the designation *Electronic* for the medium.

Delk, Cheryl L. *Discovering American Culture*. Ann Arbor: U of

    Michigan P. 1997. Berkeley Public Lib. 20 June 2006.

    Electronic.

73. Electronic Television or Radio Program

Lifson, Edward. "Clinton Meets Kohl." *Morning Edition*. 13 May 1998. Natl.

    Public Radio. Web. 7 July 2006.

74. Electronic Sound Recording or Sound Clip

Beethoven, Ludwig van. "Symphony no. 5 in C, op. 67." June 1998. New City

    Media Audio Programs. Web. 20 July 2006.

75. Electronic Film or Film Clip

Anderson, Paul Thomas, dir. *Boogie Nights*. 1997. Trailer. New Line

    Cinema. Web. 13 May 2006.

76. Online Work of Art

Van Gogh, Vincent. *The Starry Night*. 1889. Museum of Mod. Art, New York.

    Web. 20 Mar. 2006.

77. Online Interview

Gregson-Wagner, Natasha. Interview. *Hollywood Online*. May 1998. Web.

    15 May 2006.

78. Online Map

"Mellow Mountain: Park City, Utah." Map. *MapQuest*. Web. 17 Feb. 2007.

79. Online Cartoon

Trudeau. Gary. "Doonesbury." Cartoon. *New York Times*. New York

    Times, 13 May 1998. Web. 3 Dec. 2006.

80. Online Advertisement

3D RealAudio. Advertisement. Web. 20 Aug. 2006.

81. Online Manuscript or Working Paper

Hendrickson, Heather. "Art: Impractical but Essential." Working paper,

    n.d. Web. 28 Aug. 2006.

[*Note*: *n.d.* stands for "no date."]

82. Email Communication

Provide the writer's name (or alias or screen name); the subject (title) of the communication, if any (in quotation marks); the designation *message to*; the name of the person to whom the email is addressed; and the date of the message. The publication medium is listed last. [Note that *e-mail* is spelled with a hyphen in MLA style.]

Gardner, Susan. "Help with Citations." Message to the author. 20 Mar.

    2002. E-mail.

83. Online Posting

For a message posted to an email discussion list, include, in addition to the information provided for an email citation, the description *Online posting* and the date of the posting. Provide the name of the discussion list, if known. Then give the medium and the date of access. If needed to locate the post, include the URL.

Surendranath, Lindsey. "Secondary Writing Center." Online posting.

30 June 2006. WPA Discussion List. Web. 7 July 2006.

<http://wpacouncil.org>.

Citation of a posting to a World Wide Web discussion forum follows the style for an online posting.

84. Downloaded Computer Software or Digital File.

Fusion. Vers. 2.1. 30 June 2002 Digital file.

6e   Review a student research paper in MLA style

The following research paper, written by Kaycee Sorensen, is formatted according to MLA style. Annotations that explain various conventions are printed in blue.

Writer's last name   Sorensen 1
and page number
appear on every page.

Kaycee Sorensen   student

Professor Hult   professor

English 2010H   course identification

3 May 2003   date

Online Shopping: Title centered

Risky (but Better) Business

Recently, I shopped at the Logan Old Navy to find   Double
spacing
a new pair of jeans, but since I wear an uncommon size,

I could not find exactly what I wanted. The attendant in   Introduction
using appeal
the fitting rooms suggested that I visit *OldNavy.com* to find   to authority

what I was looking for. She gave me all the information I would need to find the jeans and purchase them online, and when I visited *OldNavy.com*, I found the jeans, and they were cheaper than in the store. Needless to say, I bought more than just the jeans because of the wonderful prices. This was not my first experience, but because of the price, the convenience, and access to more items, I became excited to seek out new online shopping venues.

I am not alone in my growing interest in online shopping. According to *Nielsen-Netratings*, 498 million people worldwide now have access to the Internet from home, and just as these people are using the Internet for quick access to information and electronic communication, millions of them are also turning to the Internet for shopping purposes (Hupprich and Bumatay). Consumers should shop online because, despite fears of safety and identity theft, the simplicity, convenience of comparison shopping, and access to a variety of merchandise makes online shopping the logical and best choice for consumers.

Internet source without a page number

Thesis: Main Point

The convenience of online shopping became clear to me not only as a consumer but also as a retailer. During the holidays, I work for Sears in Frisco, TX. Our store is new, and we still only serve the urban areas, so many people travel from rural areas to shop. While working over Christmas, I helped one such woman who needed to shop for items for the baby she was expecting.

[New Page]

Works Cited Alphabetical listing of all sources used

Better Business Bureau Program. 2002. Web. 22 Mar. 2003   Online: Professional site

Chan, Christine, et al. "Online Spending to Reach $10 Billion

    for Holiday Season 2001." *Nielsen-Netratings*   Title of article

    20 Nov. 2001. Web. 28 July 2002.

Cox, Beth. "E-commerce: Color It Green." *Cyberatlas*   Name of professional site

    3 Aug. 2002. Web. 12 Apr. 2003.   ←——— Date of publication

Frey, Christine. "Online Shopper: Advantages of Plastic."   Date of access

    Los Angeles Times 18 Oct. 2001: T8. Print.   Print: Newspaper

Greenspan, Robyn. "E-shopping around the World." *Cyberatlas*   Internet: Online newsletter

    5 Aug. 2002. Web. 23 Mar. 2003.

"How Encryption Works." *Netscape Security Center*. Web. 5 Apr. 2003.

Hupprich, Laura, and Maria Bumatay. "*Nielsen/Netratings* Reports

    a Record Half Billion People Worldwide Now Have Home

    Internet Access." *Nielsen-Netratings* 3 June 2002. Web. 3

    Apr. 2003.   Initial capitals are used in article titles, which are also put in quotation marks.

Kushairi, Ahmad. "The Buying Experience Is Still with Offline

    Shopping." *New Strait Times Press* 12 Aug. 2002: 2. Print.

"Nearly One-Third of Teens Make Offline Purchases after Window

    Shopping Online." *PR Newswire Association, Inc.* 18 July

    2001: Financial News Sect. *Academic Search Elite*. Web.   Library reference database: Full-text article

    Logan. 20 Mar. 2003.

"Online-Shopping Safety and Security." *Shopping Guide* 8 Aug. 2002.

    Web. 12 Apr. 2003.

Pastore, Michael. "Web Influences Offline Purchases, Especially
    among Teens." *Cyberatlas* 3 Aug. 2002. Web. 18 Mar. 2003.
Stark, Ellen. "There's Help on the Way If You Face a Credit Card
    Dispute." *Money* May 1996: 41. Print.
"Virtual Model Tech Hikes Lands' End Sales." *Capital Times* 27 Sept.
    2001: 6E. Print.

Print:
Magazine

7   APA, CMS, and CSE Documentation

This chapter provides an overview of three styles of documentation, codified
by the American Psychological Association, the *Chicago Manual of Style*, and
the Council of Science Editors.

APA STYLE

The documentation style commonly employed in the social sciences was
developed by the American Psychological Association (APA). Detailed documentation guidelines for the APA style are included in the *Publication Manual
of the American Psychological Association*, 5th ed. (Washington: APA, 2001). The
social sciences use an author-date method of documentation.

In-text citations identify the source by the author's name and the date of publication so that the reader knows immediately whether the research cited is
current. The date of publication is also emphasized in the References list at the
end of the paper.

A Directory to APA Style

(continued)

7a Integrate sources and avoid plagiarism in APA style

In Chapter 3, "Evaluating and Using Sources: Avoiding Plagiarism," we talked in general about the importance of using sources accurately and responsibly in your research papers. To help you do so, the APA citation style provides for a two-part system of source identification: (1) parenthetical references within the body of the paper (discussed in 7b), and (2) a References list at the end of the paper (discussed in 7d). By using APA style, you can integrate your source information appropriately and ethically without inadvertently committing plagiarism.

APA Citation Style

1. Introduce your source using a *signal phrase* that names its author, immediately followed by the date of publication in parentheses or include the name and date in parentheses at the end.

   `Jones (1995) states that ...` or `(Jones, 1995)`

2. Paraphrase or summarize the information from your source. It's best to use direct quotations sparingly. Recast the source information into your own words. If you do use any words or phrases from the author, however, be sure to put them in quotation marks and to provide a page number in parentheses.

   (continued)

3. If you did not name the author in a signal phrase, insert in parentheses at the conclusion of your summary the author's last name, a comma, and the date of publication:

`(Jones, 1995).`

For a direct quotation or close paraphrase, also provide a page number:

`(Jones, 1995, p. 75).`

4. At the end of your paper, list the source with complete bibliographic information on your References page.

Plagiarism, a serious academic offense, is often inadvertently committed by students in one of the following ways:

1. Failing to acknowledge a summary or paraphrase of a source in the body of the paper through a signal phrase and parenthetical citation.

2. Using the original authors' words without putting the borrowed words or phrases in quotation marks or including a parenthetical citation.

❶ Acknowledge all sources

A successful research paper will be written as an argument in the writer's own words, expressing an understanding of the answers to specific research questions. In such a paper, sources are used as evidence in support of the writer's argument. Source support is integrated into the flow of the research paper through the use of paraphrases and summaries in the writer's own words; each source is acknowledged by a parenthetical citation. Failing to acknowledge a source results in plagiarism. In addition to paraphrases and summaries, any other source material must also be acknowledged, such as specific facts, graphics or visuals, cartoons, diagrams, or charts, using the two-part APA citation system. Note that the APA system stresses the publication date of a source by including that date in the parenthetical citation along with the name of the author. This is because researchers in the social sciences want to know immediately how current the source information is.

❷ Indicate original source words and phrases with quotation marks

The best research papers use direct quotations sparingly as support for their own ideas and integrate those quotations smoothly into the flow of the paper. A signal phrase alerts the reader that a direct quotation follows; the quotation marks show exactly which words and phrases are being quoted. Long quotations are formatted using indentation rather than quotation marks. Carelessness at the note-taking stage can result in unintentional plagiarism (see 3c).

7b   APA style for in-text citations

In APA style, citations found in the body of the paper are linked to the References list at the end. Both the author's last name and the year of publication are included in the in-text citation.

1. Author Named in a signal phrase

If the author is mentioned in a signal phrase, provide the year of publication in parentheses just after the name.

```
Hacking (1995) covers much that is on public record about multiple
personality disorder.
```

2. Author Not Named in the Narrative

If the author is not mentioned in the narrative, provide the author's last name and the year of publication in parentheses at an appropriate place. Include a comma between the author's name and the date of publication.

```
In antiquity and through the Middle Ages, memory was a valued skill
(Hacking, 1995).
```

3. Specific Page or Paragraph Quoted

When quoting or directly paraphrasing the author's words, provide a page number (or a paragraph number if the electronic source includes one). Precede the page reference with the abbreviation *p.* (to cite one page), *pp.* (to cite more than one page), or the symbol ¶ or the abbreviation *para.*

There may be a causal explanation for multiple personality

disorder, because "multiplicity is strongly associated with early

and repeated child abuse, especially sexual abuse" (Hacking, 1995,

p. 73).

If the quotation from an electronic source does not have pages or paragraph numbers, provide author and year only.

Vault Reports makes the following request on its Web site: "If you work

(or have worked) for a company we write about...please fill out our

survey and tell us about your experience" (2006).

4. Work by Two Authors

In citing a work by two authors, provide the last names of both authors. Use the word *and* to separate their names in a signal phrase, but use an ampersand (&) to separate their names in an in-text parenthetical citation.

As Sullivan and Qualley (1994) point out, many recent publications take

the politics of writing instruction as their central concern.

or

The explanation for recent turmoil in the academy may be found in

politics (Sullivan & Qualley, 1994).

5. Work by More Than Two Authors

In the first reference to a work by three, four, or five authors, provide the last names for all authors. In subsequent citations, use the first author's last name and the Latin phrase *et al.* (for "and others"). When a work has six or more authors, include only the name of the first author, followed by *et al.*, in the first and all following citations.

According to Britton et al. (1975), mature writers consider their readers

more than themselves.

6. Anonymous Work

If no author's name is provided, use either the title or an abbreviated form of the title (usually the first few words) for the in-text citation. Italicize the title of a book, periodical, brochure, or report; use quotation marks around the title of an article or chapter.

Public schools have become overly dependent on the IQ test as an

indication of academic potential (*Human Abilities*, 1988).

An individual's success in life depends in large measure on the cultural

context in which he or she was raised ("Beyond IQ," 1994).

7. Work by a Corporate Author

Generally, provide the full name of a corporate author in in-text parenthetical citations.

Recently published statistics show the gap between the rich and poor to

be widening (New York Times Company, 2005).

If the name of the corporate author is long (such as United Cerebral Palsy Association) or if its abbreviation is easily recognized (such as APA), use the abbreviation after including both the complete name and the abbreviation in the first text reference.

8. Works by Authors with the Same Last Name

When the reference list includes two or more primary authors with the same last name, provide those authors' initials in all citations, even if the publication dates are different.

G. A. Fraser (2001) writes about abuse as the cause of multiple

personality disorder.

S. Fraser (1997) has written a memoir about incest and its effect on

multiplicity.

9. Two or More Sources

To cite several different sources within the same parenthetical citation, list the sources in alphabetical order by the authors' names, and use a semicolon to separate the entries.

Several studies (Prinsky & Rosenbaum, 1987; Record Labeling, 1985;

Thigpen, 1993) show concern about songs with themes of drugs and violence.

10. Personal Communication

Personal correspondence, such as letters, telephone conversations, lecture notes, and email, should be cited only in the text itself. Do not list the communications on the References page because readers cannot access them. Provide the initials and the last name of the correspondent, the designation *personal communication*, and the date.

J. Tompkins suggests that fear of authority prevents true learning in

elementary, secondary, college, and university classrooms (personal

communication, August 7, 2004).

11. Web Sites

When referring to an entire Web site (as opposed to a specific document or page on the site), it is sufficient in APA style to give the address of the Web site in the text. Such a reference is not included on the References page. (Note that *home page* is spelled as two words in APA style.)

Patricia Jarvis's home page includes a great deal of information about

recent archaeological digs in the Great Basin (http://www.asu.edu/

~students).

7c   APA style for content notes

The APA discourages use of content notes. They should be included only if they enhance or strengthen the discussion. Number notes consecutively throughout the text, using a superscript number. List the notes on a separate Notes page at the end of the text.

7d   APA style for the References list

The research paper's References page (the equivalent of the Works Cited list in MLA style) contains an alphabetical listing of all the works used as sources. The purpose of the References list is to help readers find the materials used in writing the paper, so the entries must be complete and accurate. List sources alphabetically by the last name of the author. When no author is given, alphabetize by the first word of the title (ignoring *A, An,* or *The*). Format the References list in a paper according to the APA style for a final text: type the first word of each entry at the left margin, and indent subsequent lines of the same entry five spaces (or one-half inch). Double-space the entire References page, both between and within entries.

Books   A citation for a book has four basic parts:

Author's Name. (Publication Date). *Title of work.* Publication Information.

Begin a book citation with the author's last name, followed by a comma and the first and middle initials. Initials are followed by a period and a word space. Next, give the year of publication, enclosed in parentheses and followed by a period. Italicize the title and subtitle of the book. (Separate them with a colon.) Capitalize the first word of the title and the first word of the subtitle, as well as any proper nouns. Follow the title with publication information: the city of publication and the publisher, separated from each other with a colon. If the city is not well known or could be confused with another city, include a state or country abbreviation. Omit the word *Publisher* and abbreviations such as *Inc.* and *Co.* from the publisher's name. Include the complete names of university presses and associations. (For guidelines on citing books in electronic format, see item 32.)

1. Book by One Author

Bolick, C. (1988). *Changing course: Civil rights at the crossroads.*

New Brunswick. NJ: Transaction Books.

2. Book by Two or More Authors

When a book has two to six authors, provide all the authors' names (last name first, followed by initials) in the order in which they appear on the title page. This order may not be alphabetical. Connect the final two names with an ampersand (&). Abbreviate the seventh and subsequent authors as *et al.*

Hindelang, M. J., Hirschi, T., & Weis, J. G. (1981). *Measuring*

delinquency. Beverly Hills, CA: Sage.

3. Book by a Corporate Author

Begin the entry with the full name of the group; alphabetize the entry by the first important word in the name. Should the same group be listed as author and publisher, use the word *Author* at the end of the entry in place of the publisher's name.

National Commission on Excellence in Education. (1984). *A nation at*

risk: The full account. Cambridge, MA: USA Research.

4. Book with an Editor

For an edited book, provide the editor's name in place of an author's name. Include the abbreviation *Ed.* (for "Editor") or *Eds.* (for "Editors") in parentheses immediately following the editor's name.

Aronson, M. K. (Ed.). (1988). *Understanding Alzheimer's disease:*

What it is, how to cope with it, future directions. New York,

NY: Scribner's.

5. Chapter or Selection from an Edited Book

Start with the author's name, the year of publication, and the title of the selection. Do not italicize the chapter or selection title or enclose it in quotation marks. Next, provide the names of the editors in normal order as they appear on the title page, preceded by the word *In* and followed by the abbreviation *Ed.* or *Eds.* (in parentheses). End the entry with the book's title (italicized), the inclusive page numbers for the selection (in parentheses), and the publication information.

Kadushin, A. (1988). Neglect in families. In E. W. Nunnally,

C. S. Chilman, & F. M. Cox (Eds.), *Mental illness,*

delinquency, addiction, and neglect (pp. 147-166).

Newbury Park, CA: Sage.

6. Two or More Books by the Same Author

Arrange the entries by the date of publication, with the earliest first. If you have two or more works by the same author published in the same year, alphabetize by title and distinguish the entries by adding a lowercase letter immediately after the year: (1991a), (1991b).

Flynn, J. R. (1980). *Race, IQ, and Jensen*. London: Routledge.

Flynn, J. R. (1991). *Asian Americans: Achievement beyond IQ.*

Hillsdale, NJ: Erlbaum.

7. Article in a Reference Book

If an encyclopedia entry is signed, start with the author's name; if it is unsigned, start with the title of the article. The publication date follows the author's name or, if no author's name is given, the title of the article. Provide the volume number and page numbers of the article (in parentheses) after the title of the reference book.

Davidoff, L. (1984). Childhood psychosis. In *The encyclopedia of*

psychology (Vol. 10, pp. 156-157). New York: Wiley.

8. Book in Translation

Indicate the name of the translator in parentheses after the book's title, with the abbreviation *Trans.*

Freire, P. (1993). *Pedagogy of the oppressed* (New rev. 20th anniv.

ed., M. B. Ramos, Trans.). New York: Continuum.

9. Subsequent Edition of a Book

If a book is not a first edition, indicate the relevant edition in parentheses immediately following the title of the book. Use abbreviations to specify the type of edition: for example, *2nd ed.* stands for "Second edition" and *Rev. ed.* stands for "Revised edition."

Lindeman, E. (2005). *A rhetoric for writing teachers* (4th ed.). New

York: Oxford University Press.

10. Republished Book

Provide the original date of publication in parentheses at the end of the entry, with the words *Original work published.*

Dewey, J. (1963). *Experience and education*. New York: Collier.

(Original work published 1938)

11. Government Document

Unless an author's name is given, begin an entry for a government document with the name of the agency that issued the publication.

National Center for Educational Statistics. (2006). *The condition

of education*, 2006. Washington, DC: U.S. Department of

Education, Office of Educational Research and Improvement.

12. Published Proceedings from a Conference

Van Belle, J. G. (2002). Online interaction: Learning communities

in the virtual classroom. In J. Chambers (Ed.), *Selected

papers from the 13th International Conference on College*

Teaching and Learning (pp. 187-200). Jacksonville, FL:

Community College at Jacksonville Press.

13. One Volume of a Multivolume Work

Doyle, A. C. (1930). *The complete Sherlock Holmes* (Vol. 2). Garden

City, NY: Doubleday.

Periodicals   A citation of an article in a periodical or a journal follows a format similar to that for a book:

Author's name. (Publication date). Article title. Publication information.

When citing magazines and newpapers, include the month and date of publication. The article title and subtitle appear without quotation marks or italics. The publication information begins with the name of the publication as it appears on the publication's title page, with all major words capitalized. Italicize the journal name. Include the volume number (italicized and not preceded by the abbreviation *vol.*) and the issue number (in parentheses and not italicized) if available, regardless of whether the journal is paginated separately by issue or continuously by volume. End with the inclusive page numbers for the article. (Use the abbreviation *p.* or *pp.* with articles in newspapers but not with articles in journals or magazines.) (For guidelines on citing articles in online periodicals, see items 33–40.)

14. Article in a Journal

```
            Publication
  Author      date                Article Title              Article subtitle
┌─────────┐┌───────┐┌──────────────────────────────────┐┌──────────────┐
Popenoe, D. (1993). American family decline, 1960-1990: A review

    and appraisal. Journal of Marriage and Family, 55(3), 527-555.
   └──────────────┘└──────────────────────────────────────────────┘
                              Publication information
```

15. Article in a Monthly Magazine

Include the month, not abbreviated, following the year in the publication date.

Dobson, L. (2006, July/August). What's your humor style? *Psychology*

    Today, 48.

16. Article in a Weekly Magazine

Provide the year, month, and day of publication.

Ratliff, E. (2006, July 2). Déjà vu, again and again. *The New York*

    Times Magazine, 38.

    If the article has no known author, start the entry with the title of the article, and alphabetize by the first important word in the title (usually the word that follows the introductory article).

The blood business. (1972, September 7). *Time*, 47–48.

    In the References list, this entry would appear in the B's.

17. Newspaper Article

    Provide the complete name of the newspaper (including any introductory articles) after the title of the article. List all discontinuous page numbers, preceded by *pp.*

Pollack, A. (2006, July 13). Paralyzed man uses thoughts to move a

    cursor. *The New York Times*, pp. A1, A21.

18. Editorial

    Add the word *Editorial*, in brackets, after the title.

Madigan, C. (2006, July 13). Is the Web changing journalism?

    [Editorial]. *The Chicago Tribune*, p. A23.

19. Letter to the Editor

    Add the designation *Letter to the editor*, in brackets, after the title of the letter or after the date if there is no title.

Fischer, S. (2006, July 13). [Letter to the editor]. *The New York*

    Times, p. A22.

20. Review

Provide the name of the reviewer, the date of publication (in parentheses), and the title of the review, if given. Then, in brackets, write the designation *Review of* and the title of the piece that was reviewed.

Ribadeneira, D. (1997, October 31). The secret lives of seminarians

    [Review of the book *The new men: Inside the Vatican's elite*

    school for American priests]. *The Boston Globe*, p. C6.

21. Unsigned Article

Quacks in European solidarity. (2002, August). *The Economist*, 50.

22. More Than One Work by the Same Author in the Same Year

List the works alphabetically by title, and use lowercase letters after the dates to distinguish the works.

Hayles, N. K. (1996a). Inside the teaching machine: Actual feminism

    and (virtual) pedagogy. *The Electronic Journal for Computer*

    Writing, Rhetoric and Literature, 2. Retrieved from http:/

    /www.cwrl.utexas.edu/cwrl

Hayles, N. K. (1996b). Self/subject. In P. Vandenberg & P. Heilker

    (Eds.), *Keywords in composition* (pp. 217-220). Portsmouth, NH:

    Heinemann/Boynton-Cook.

Other Sources

23. Film or Video Recording

Begin with the names of those responsible for the film and, in parentheses, their titles, such as *Producer* and *Director*. Give the title (italicized), and then designate the medium in brackets. Provide the location and name of the distributor.

Ossana, D. (Producer), & Lee, A. (Director). (2005). *Brokeback Mountain*

    [Motion picture]. United States: Focus Features.

24. Television or Radio Program

Identify those who created the program, and give their titles—for example, *Producer, Director,* and *Anchor.* Give the date the program was broadcast. Provide the program's title (italicized), as well as the city and the station where the program aired.

Miller, R. (Producer). (1982, May 21). *Problems of freedom.* New

York: NBC-TV.

25. Technical Report

Write an entry for a technical report in a format similar to that for a book. If an individual author is named, provide that information; place any other identifying information (such as a report number) after the title of the report.

Vaughn Hansen Associates, in association with CH2M Hill and Water

Research Laboratory, Utah State University. (1995).

Identification and assessment of certain water management

options for the Wasatch Front: Prepared for Utah State

Division of Water Resources. Salt Lake City, UT: Author.

26. Published Interview

For a published interview, start with the name of the interviewer and the date. In brackets, give the name (and title, if necessary) of the person interviewed. End with the publication information, including the page or pages in parentheses, after the title of the work in which the interview was published.

Davidson, P. (1992). [Interview with Donald Hall]. In P. Davidson,

The fading smile (p. 25). New York: Knopf.

27. Unpublished Interview

Follow the format for a published interview.

Hult, C. A. (1997, March). [Interview with Dr. Stanford Cazier,

past president, Utah State University].

28. Unpublished Dissertation

Provide the author's name, the date, and then the title of the dissertation, italicized and followed by a period. Add the phrase *Unpublished doctorial dissertation*, a comma, and the name of the degree-granting institution.

Johnson, N. K. (1980). *Cultural and psychological determinants of health and*

    illness. Unpublished doctoral dissertation, University of Washington.

29. Speech or Lecture

For an oral presentation, provide the name of the presenter, the year and month of the presentation, and the title of the presentation (italicized). Then give any useful location information.

Meeks, L. L. (1997, March 3). *Feminism and the WPA.* Speech given at the

    Conference on College Composition and Communication, Phoenix, AZ.

30. Paper Presented at a Conference

Provide information about the location of the meeting as well as the month in which the meeting was held.

Klaus, C. (1996, March). *Teachers and writers.* Paper presented at the

    meeting of the Conference on College Composition and Communication,

    Milwaukee, WI.

Electronic Media The fifth edition of the *Publication Manual of the American Psychological Association* (2001) was updated in 2007 with new formats for electronic documentation, as shown in the following examples. When citing electronic media, use the standard APA format to identify authorship, date of origin (if known), and title, much as for print material; electronic retrieval information is placed at the end of the reference. If you are referencing an electronic version that duplicates a print source exactly, simply use the basic journal reference format for print sources. Indicate the

WebLink
http://www.apa.org
The official Web site of the American Psychological Association.

electronic version by including [Electronic version] in brackets immediately following the article's title.

31. Online Professional or Personal Site

To comply with APA style, present information in the following general sequence when citing online sources:

1. The author's or editor's last name and initials

2. The creation date of the work, in parentheses; use *n.d.* (no date) if the electronic publication date is not available

3. The title of the complete work, italicized

4. The relevant subpage (if the document is contained within a large, complex site)

5. The word *Retrieved*, followed by the date and a comma, followed by the word *from* and the site title

6. The access protocol or path or URL (Note: Break URL lines only before a slash or a period; do not follow the URL with a period.)

7. When a Digital Object Identifier (DOI) is available, use the DOI instead of the URL in the reference

```
McCarthy, B. (1997). Reflections on the past--Antiques. Retrieved January

    20, 1998, from Resources for Victorian Living Web site: http://www

    .victoriana.com
```

32. Online Book

Provide any data on the print publication before giving details on where the electronic version can be located.

```
Aristotle. (1954). Rhetoric (W. R. Roberts, Trans.). Retrieved from The

    English Server at Carnegie Mellon University: http://www.rpi.edu

    /~honeyl/Rhetoric/index.html
```

NOTE No retrieval date is necessary when content is not likely to change, as for a published article or book.

33. Article in an Online Work

Generally, citations for articles in online works follow the same sequence as citations for their print counterparts, followed by the retrieval statement.

Women in American history. (2007). In *Encyclopaedia Britannica*. Retrieved

   from http://www.women.eb.com

34. Article in an Online Newspaper or on a Newswire

Green, T. (2006, July 10). The Air and Space Museum is falling. *The Los*

   Angeles Times. Retrieved from http://latimes.com

35. Article in an Online Magazine

Fantino, J. (2004, March). Crime prevention: Are we missing the mark?

   The Police Chief Magazine. Retrieved from http://

   policechiefmagazine.org

36. Online Review

Donnelly, P. (2005). Women and patients [Review of the book *Female*

   solution]. *OBGYN.net*. Retrieved from http://www.obgyn.net

   /women/women.asp

37. Online Abstract

Gould, M. (2006). Seven ways to improve student satisfaction in online

   classes. *Distance Education Report, 10*(12), 7. Abstract retrieved

   from Academic Search Premier database.

38. Online Editorial

Rao, L. (2006, August). Do you know your vitamins and minerals?

   [Editorial]. *Prevention*. Retrieved from http://www.prevention.com

39. Online Letter to the Editor

Masek, T. (2006, July 10). Dirty tricks and fraud [Letter to the editor].

   The Salt Lake Tribune. Retrieved from http://www.sltrib.com

40. Article in an Online Scholarly Journal (with Digital Object Identifier)

Brumfiel, G. (2006). Planet hunters seek cheap missions. *Nature, 442*

(7098), 6. doi: 10.1038/442006a

41. Document or Full-Text Article Found via a Reference Database

To cite a full-text article you derive from a service that your library subscribes to (e.g., *LexisNexis, EBSCOhost,* or *ProQuest*), follow the citation for the source itself (the same as for its print counterpart) with the name of the service (itacized) and the library.

King, M. (2000, July 6). Companies here ponder Scout ruling. *Seattle*

Times, A1. *LexisNexis*. Utah State University Library, Logan.

42. Nonperiodical Publication on CD-ROM or Disc

ClearVue, Inc. (2007). *The history of European literature* [CD-ROM].

Chicago: Author.

43. Online Work of Art

Seurat, G. (1884). *A Sunday on La Grande Jatte.* Art Institute of Chicago.

Retrieved from http://www.artic.edu/aic/collections

44. Online Interview

Buckley, T. (2006, July 11). Jazz ready for Fisher [Interview with Jerry

Sloan]. *Deseret News.* Retrieved from http://www.desnews.com

45. Online Posting

Although unretrievable communication such as email is not included in APA References, public or retrievable Internet postings from newsgroups or electronic mailing lists may be included.

Walker, J. (2006, April 17). 2006 graduate research network and

travel awards. *Appalachian Alliance for Computers and Writing*

Discussion List. Retrieved from http://www.kcte.org/hypermail/aacw-L/

archive.200604/0000.html

7e   Review a student research report in APA style

The following research paper, written by two students in a general education course, is formatted according to the APA style of documentation. Annotations that explain various conventions appear in color.

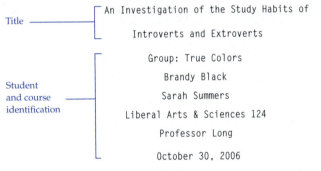

Title page   Shortened title appears with   Introverts and Extroverts   1
                  page number on every page

                  Running Head: INTROVERTS AND EXTROVERTS
                  If the paper is being submitted for publication, include the shortened
                  title to be used as a header on every page of the printed version

Title ———   An Investigation of the Study Habits of

                      Introverts and Extroverts

                          Group: True Colors
                            Brandy Black
Student   Sarah Summers
and course
identification   Liberal Arts & Sciences 124
                           Professor Long

                          October 30, 2006

                  An abstract, a brief summary of the
                  paper, is often included as the second
                  page in social science papers.

            An Investigation of the Study Habits of   Title
                  Introverts and Extroverts

        Research about personality types and their study habits has   Double-
                                                                          spaced text
become increasingly important. In particular, psychologists have

studied how to recognize personality types of students and how to

Introverts and Extroverts 2

teach different kinds of students. Because of this national interest, we decided to investigate the study habits of two personality types, introverts and extroverts. We began this study with two general assumptions. First, we thought that introverts would be less socially active in their study habits, spend more time studying, and have a higher degree of academic success. Second, we thought that extroverts would study in groups, study less, and have slightly lower grades. In order to investigate our assumptions, we read several articles in journals such as *Psychological Reports, Personality and Individual Differences,* and *The Journal of Research in Personality.*

— Hypothesis

— Background information

We constructed a four-page survey about academic success and study habits, which we asked 15 students to answer. In addition, we also created a 6-day study log to chart the length of study time, duration of breaks, and types of studying done by the students. The purpose of this research report is to review the literature and to present information from our own research. This report shows that our own research, for the most part, replicated the findings of many of the national studies. Information in this paper will be presented in two sections. First, findings from the larger, national studies will be summarized. Then, findings from our study will follow.

— Thesis

Other's research is reviewed and summarized in the literature review

Literature Review

According to national studies, there are three major trends used in tracing the academic life of extroverts and introverts....

[New Page]   APA citation style

                                        Introverts and Extroverts 6

Only first word and proper nouns are
capitalized in article or book title

Initials ⟶   References

Campbell, J. B. (1983). Differential relationships of extroversion,

impassivity, and sociability to study habits. *Journal of* — Publication date

Research in Personality, 17(3), 308-313 ⟵ Page numbers

Campbell, J. B., & Hawley, C. W. (1982). Study habits and Eysenck's

theory of extroversion-introversion. *Journal of Research in* Journal name,
in capital and
lowercase

Personality, 16(2), 139-146. letters, is
italicized

Furnham, A., & Medhurst, S. (1995). Personality correlates of

academic seminar behavior: A study of four instruments. No quotation
marks around
title

Personality and Individual Differences, 19(2), 197-208.

Irfani, S. (1978). Extroversion-introversion and self-rated Volume number

academic success. *Psychological Reports, 43*(2), 508-510. is italicized

Olympia, D. E., Sheridan, S. M., Jenson, W. R., & Andrews, D. Internet
journal

(1994). Using student-managed interventions to increase

homework completion and accuracy. *Journal of Applied Behavior*

Analysis, 27(1), 85-99. Retrieved from http://www.envmed

.rochester.edu/www.rap/behavior/jaba.htm

CMS STYLE

The documentation style used most commonly in business, communications, economics, and the humanities and fine arts (other than languages and literature) is outlined in *The Chicago Manual of Style*, 15th ed. (Chicago: University of Chicago

Press, 2003). The two-part CMS style typically uses footnotes or endnotes and a bibliography to provide publication information about sources quoted, paraphrased, summarized, or otherwise referred to in the text of a paper. Footnotes appear at the bottom of the page; endnotes appear on a separate page at the end of the

http://www.press.uchicago.edu/
Misc/Chicago/cmosfaq.html
For answers to questions about
CMS style

WebLink

paper. The Bibliography, like the Works Cited page in MLA style, is an alphabetical list of all works cited in the paper.

7f Integrate sources and avoid plagiarism in CMS style

In Chapter 3, "Evaluating and Using Sources: Avoiding Plagiarism," we talked in general about the importance of using sources accurately and responsibly in your research papers. To help you do so, the CMS citation format provides for a two-part system of source identification: (1) footnote superscript numbers and footnotes within the body of the paper (discussed in 7g and 7h), and (2) a Bibliography at the end of the paper (discussed in 7i). By using CMS style, you can integrate your source information appropriately and ethically without inadvertently committing plagiarism.

CMS Citation Style

1. Introduce your source using a *signal phrase* that names its author, with a superscript footnote number following the source information:

   ... according to Calvin Jones.[1]

2. Paraphrase or summarize the information from your source. It's best to use direct quotations sparingly. Rather, recast the source information into your own words. If you do use any words or phrases from the author, however, be sure to put them in quotation marks.

   (continued)

3. Format your footnotes (which are listed on the page on which the source was cited) or endnotes (which are typed in one consecutive list at the end of the paper before the bibliography) according to CMS style.
4. At the end of your paper, list the source with complete bibliographic information on your Bibliography page.

Plagiarism, a serious academic offense, is often inadvertently committed by students in one of the following ways:

1. Failing to acknowledge a summary or paraphrase of a source in the body of the paper through a signal phrase and footnote number.

2. Using the original authors' words without putting the borrowed words or phrases in quotation marks or including a footnote number.

❶ Acknowledge all sources

A successful research paper will be written as an argument in the writer's own words, expressing an understanding of the answers to specific research questions. In such a paper, sources are used as evidence in support of the writer's argument. Source support is integrated into the flow of the research paper through the use of paraphrases and summaries in the writer's own words; each source is acknowledged by a footnote. Failing to acknowledge a source results in plagiarism. In addition to paraphrases and summaries, any other source material must also be acknowledged, such as specific facts, graphics or visuals, cartoons, diagrams, or charts, using CMS citation style.

❷ Indicate original source words and phrases with quotation marks

The best research papers use direct quotations sparingly as support for their own ideas and integrate those quotations smoothly into the flow of the paper. A signal phrase alerts the reader that a direct quotation follows; the quotation marks show exactly which words and phrases are being quoted. Long quotations are formatted using indentation rather than quotation marks. Carelessness at the note-taking stage can result in unintentional plagiarism (see 3c).

CMS style for in-text citations

In the text, indicate a note with a superscript number typed immediately after the information that is being referenced. Number notes consecutively throughout the text.

> In *A History of Reading*, Alberto Manguel asserts that "we, today's readers, have yet to learn what reading is."[1] As a result, one of his conclusions is that while readers have incredible powers, not all of them are enlightening.[2]

 CMS style for notes

For footnotes, position the text of the note at the bottom of the page on which the reference occurs. Separate the footnotes from the text by skipping four lines from the last line of text. Single-space within a note, but double-space between notes if more than one note appears on a page.

For endnotes, type all of the notes at the end of the paper, in a section titled Notes. The title, centered but not in quotation marks, should appear at the top of the first page of the notes. List the notes in consecutive order, as they occur in the text. Double-space the entire endnote section—between and within entries.

The other details of formatting are the same for both footnotes and endnotes. Indent the first line of each note five spaces (or one-half inch). Use a number that is the same size as and is aligned in the same way as the note text (do not use a superscript); follow the number with a period and a word space to the note itself. Begin with the author's name (first name first), followed by a comma. Then provide the title of the book (italicized) or article (enclosed in quotation marks). Finally, provide the publication information. For books, include (in parentheses) the place of publication, followed by a colon; the publisher, followed by a comma; and the date of publication. Conclude with the page number of the source, preceded by a comma. For articles, include the title of the periodical (italicized), followed by the volume or issue number. Then add the date of publication (in parentheses), followed by a colon and the page number.

Book

1. Alberto Manguel, *A History of Reading* (New York: Viking, 1996), 23.

Article

2. Steven Brachlow, "John Robinson and the Lure of Separatism in Pre-Revolutionary England," *Church History* 50 (1983): 288-301.

In subsequent references to the same source, the *Chicago Manual* recommends using a short form including the author's last name, a shortened title, and a page number:

(Short Form) 3. Manguel, *History of Reading*, 289.

The abbreviation *ibid.* (in the same place) is used to refer to a single work referenced in the immediately preceding note. If the page numbers are different, include the page number as well.

4. Ibid., 291.

5. Ibid.

Books

1. Book by One Author

5. Iris Murdoch. *The Sovereignty of Good* (New York: Schocken Books, 1971), 32-33.

(Short Form) 5. Murdoch, *Sovereignty*, 33.

2. Book by Two or Three Authors

List the authors' names in the same order as on the title page of the book.

6. Anne S. Goodsell, Michelle R. Maher, and Vincent Tinto, *Collaborative Learning: A Sourcebook for Higher Education* (University Park, Pa.: National Center on Postsecondary Teaching. Learning, and Assessment, 1992), 78.

3. Book by More Than Three Authors

In the long form, list all authors; in the short form, use the abbreviation *et al.* after the first author's name.

7. James Britton, Tony Burgess, Nancy Martin, Alex McLeod, and Harold Rosen, *The Development of Writing Abilities* (London: Macmillan, 1975), 43.

(Short Form) 7. Britton et al., *Development*, 43.

4. Book by a Corporate Author

8. American Association of Colleges and Universities, *American Pluralism and the College Curriculum: Higher Education in a Diverse Democracy* (Washington, D.C.: American Association of Higher Education, 1995), 27.

5. Book with an Editor

9. Jane Roberta Cooper, ed., *Reading Adrienne Rich: Review and Re-Visions, 1951-1981* (Ann Arbor: University of Michigan Press, 1984), 51.

6. Book with an Editor and an Author

10. Albert Schweitzer, *Albert Schweitzer: An Anthology*, ed. Charles R. Joy (New York: Harper & Row, 1947), 107.

7. Chapter or Selection from an Edited Work

11. Gabriele Taylor, "Gossip as Moral Talk," in *Good Gossip*, ed. Robert F. Goodman and Aaron Ben-Ze'ev (Lawrence: Kansas University Press, 1994), 35-37.

8. Article in a Reference Book

The publication information (city of publication, publisher, publication year) is usually omitted from citations of well-known reference books.

Include the abbreviation *s. v.* (*sub verbo,* or "under the word") before the article title, rather than page numbers.

    12. Frank E. Reynolds, *World Book Encyclopedia*, 1983 ed.,

s. v. "Buddhism."

9. Introduction, Preface, Foreword, or Afterword

    13. Jane Tompkins, preface to *A Life in School: What the Teacher Learned* (Reading, Mass.: Addison-Wesley, 1996), xix.

10. Work in More Than One Volume

    14. Arthur Conan Doyle, *The Complete Sherlock Holmes*, vol. 2 (Garden City, N.Y.: Doubleday, 1930), 728.

11. Government Document

    15. United States, Federal Bureau of Investigation, *Uniform Crime Reports for the United States, 1995* (Washington, D.C.: Government Printing Office, 1995), 48.

Periodicals

12. Article in a Journal Paginated by Volume (may omit issue number)

    16. Mike Rose, "The Language of Exclusion: Writing Instruction at the University," *College English* 47 (1985): 343.

(Short Form) 16. Rose, "Language of Exclusion," 343.

13. Article in a Journal Paginated by Issue (include issue number)

    17. Joy S. Ritchie, "Confronting the 'Essential' Problem: Reconnecting Feminist Theory and Pedagogy," *Journal of Advanced Composition* 10, no. 2 (1989): 160.

14. Article in a Monthly Magazine

18. Douglas H. Lamb and Glen D. Reeder, "Reliving Golden Days," *Psychology Today*, June 1986, 22.

15. Article in a Weekly Magazine

19. Steven Levy, "Blaming the Web," *Newsweek*, April 7, 1997, 46-47.

16. Newspaper Article

20. P. Ray Baker, "The Diagonal Walk," *Ann Arbor News*, June 16, 1928, sec. A. p. 2.

17. Abstract from an Abstracts Journal

21. Nancy K. Johnson, "Cultural and Psychological Determinants of Health and Illness" (Ph.D. diss., University of Washington, 1980), abstract in *Dissertation Abstracts International* 40 (1980): 425B.

Other Sources

18. Speech or Lecture

22. Wayne Booth, "Ethics and the Teaching of Literature," (paper presented to the College Forum at the 87th Annual Convention of the National Council of Teachers of English, Detroit, Mich., November 21, 1997).

19. Personal Letter to the Author

23. George H. W. Bush, letter to the author, September 8, 1995.

Electronic Media   In general, electronic sources are cited much as print sources are cited. The URL is listed at the end of the citation and is not placed in angle brackets. The *Chicago Manual* points out that dates of access are of limited usefulness because of the changeable nature of sources and suggests using the date of access only in fields where the information is particularly time-sensitive, such as medicine or law. If an access date is needed, place it in parentheses following the URL, as in item 20.

20. Article in an Online Journal

24. Ruthe Catolico Ashley, "Creating the Ideal Lawyer," *New Lawyer*, April 3, 2003, http://www.abanet.org/genpractice/newlawyer/april03/ideal .html (accessed July 20, 2003).

21. Online Professional or Personal Site

25. Academic Info., 1998-2000, "Humanities," http://www.academicinfo .net/index.html

26. Michelle Traylor, "Michelle Traylor Data Services," 1989-2002, http://www.mtdsnet.com

27. John C. Herz, "Surfing on the Internet: A Nethead's Adventures Online," *Urban Desires* 1.3, March-April 1995, http://www.desires.com

7i　CMS style for bibliography entries

For a short paper, it is not essential to provide a bibliography since your footnotes already contain the complete bibliographic information. However, if your teacher requires a bibliography, check to see if using the MLA style for a Works Cited page as outlined in Chapter 6 will be acceptable. For exact CMS bibliographic style, you will need to refer to Chapter 17 of the *Chicago Manual*.

CSE STYLE

Although source citations in the sciences are generally similar to those recommended by the APA, there is no uniform system of citation in the sciences. Various disciplines follow either the style of a particular journal or the style outlined in a style guide, such as the guide produced by the Council of Science Editors: *Scientific Style and Format: The CSE Manual for Authors, Editors, and Publishers*, 7th ed. (New York: Rockefeller University Press, 2006).

The Council of Science Editors (CSE), originally known as the Council of Biology Editors (CBE), was established in 1957 by joint action of the National Science Foundation and the American Institute of Biological Sciences. More information about the organization can be found at its Web site.

> http://councilscienceeditors.org
> The official Web site of the Council of Science Editors
> **WebLink**

7j   Integrate sources and avoid plagiarism in CSE style

In Chapter 3, "Evaluating and Using Sources: Avoiding Plagiarism," we talked in general about the importance of using sources accurately and responsibly in your research papers. To help you do so, the CSE citation format provides for a two-part system of source identification: (1) parenthetical references or reference numbers within the body of the paper (discussed in 7k), and (2) a References list that is either alphabetical or numerical at the end of the paper (discussed in 7l). By using CSE style, you can integrate your source information appropriately and ethically without inadvertently committing plagiarism. Because the CSE citation style closely resembles APA style, for more on integrating sources and avoiding plagiarism please see the information in 7a.

7k   CSE style for in-text citations

The CSE style of documentation offers three alternative formats for in-text citations: the name-year (or author-year) style, the number (or citation-sequence) style, and the citation-name style.

> http://www.wisc.edu/writing/
> Handbook/DocCBE.html
> A basic outline of the CSE's name-year system for in-text citation
> **WebLink**

Name-Year Style   If the author's name is used to introduce the source material, include only the publication date in the citation.

> According to Allen (1997), frequency of interactions and context of
>
> occurrence were unknown.

> or

> Frequency of interactions and context of occurrence were unknown
>
> (Allen 1997).

Note that there is no comma between author and year in CSE style.

Number Style In the number or citation-sequence style, numbers are assigned to the various sources, according to the sequence in which the sources are initially cited in the text. Then the sources are listed by number on the References page. Set citation numbers within the text as superscripts.

> Temperature plays a major role in the rate of gastric juice
>
> secretion.[3]

Multiple sources are cited together:

> Recent studies[3,5,8-10] show that antibodies may also bind to microbes
>
> and prevent their attachment to epithelial surfaces.

Citation-Name Style The citation-name style is the system used by the CSE manual. A complete alphabetical reference list is created and numbered, and the number for each source is inserted into the text as a superscript number next to any material that cites the source. The models below use the citation-name style.

71   CSE style for the References list

The CSE's listing of references contains all the sources cited in the paper. The title of this page may be References or Cited References. Because the purpose of this list is to help readers find the materials used in writing the paper, information must be complete and accurate.

The format of the References page will depend on which style is used. Since the References page for the name-year system basically resembles the

APA References page discussed in 7d, we will consider here the References page for the citation-name style.

Double-space the entire References list, both between and within entries. Type the citation number, followed by a period, flush left on the margin. Leave two word spaces to the first letter of the entry. Align any turn lines on the first letter of the entry. List the citations in alphabetical order.

List authors with last names first, followed by initials. Capitalize only the first word of a title and any proper nouns. Do not enclose titles of articles in quotation marks, and do not italicize titles of books or journals. Abbreviate names of journals, where possible. Include the year of publication. Cite volume and page numbers when appropriate.

Books Using Citation-Name Style

1. Book by One Author

1. Kruuk H. The spotted hyena: a study of predation and social behavior. Chicago: University of Chicago Pr; 1972.

2. Abercrombie MLJ. The anatomy of judgment. Harmondsworth (Eng.): Penguin; 1969.

2. Book by Two or More Authors

3. Hersch RH, Paolitto DP, Reimer J. Promoting moral growth. New York: Longman; 1979.

3. Book by a Corporate Author

4. Carnegie Council on Policy Studies in Higher Education. Fair practices in higher education: rights and responsibilities of students and their colleges in a period of intensified competition for enrollment. San Francisco: Jossey-Bass; 1979.

4. Book with Two or More Editors

5. Buchanan RE, Gibbons NE, editors. Bergey's manual of determinative bacteriology. 8th ed. Baltimore: Williams & Wilkins; 1974.

5. Chapter or Selection from an Edited Work

6. Kleiman DG, Brady CA. Coyote behavior in the context of recent canid research: problems and perspectives. In: Bekoff M, editor. Coyotes: biology, behavior, and management. New York: Academic Pr; 1978. pp. 163-88.

6. Government Document

7. Mech D. The wolves of Isle Royal. National Parks fauna series. Available from: United States GPO, Washington; 1966.

Periodicals

7. Journal Article by One Author

8. Schenkel R. Expression studies of wolves. Behavior 1947; 1:81-129.

8. Journal Article by Two or More Authors

9. Sargeant AB, Allen SH. Observed interactions between coyotes and red foxes. J. Mamm. 1989; 70:631-3.

9. Article with No Identified Author

10. Anonymous. Frustrated hamsters run on their wheels. Nat. Sci. 1981; 91:407.

10. Newspaper Article

11. Rensberger B, Specter B. CFCs may be destroyed by natural process. Washington Post 1989 Aug 7; Sect 1A: 2 (col 5).

11. Magazine Article

12. Aveni AF. Emissaries to the stars: the astronomers of ancient Maya. Mercury 1995 May: 15-8.

Electronic Media   Internet formats are covered in *Scientific Style and Format: The CSE Manual for Authors, Editors, and Publishers*, 7th ed.

12. Online Professional or Personal Site

13. Gelt J. Home use of greywater: rainwater conserves water-and money [Internet]. 1993

http://www.nlm.nih.gov/pubs/formats/internet.pdf
A Web document summarizing this style for Internet formats

WebLink

[cited 1996 Nov 8]. Available from: http://www.ag.arizona.edu/AZWATER/arroyo/071.rain.html

13. Online Book

14. Merck. The Merck index on-line [monograph on the Internet]. 10th ed. Rahway (NJ): Merck; 1972 [cited 1990 Dec 7]. Available from: http://www.merck.com/pubs

14. Article in an Online Periodical

15. Lechner DE, Bradbury SF, Bradley LA. Phys Ther J [serial on the Internet]. 1998 Aug [cited 1998 Sept 15]. Available from: http://www.apta.org/pt_journal/Aug98/Toc.htm

part

3

Design, Web Sites, and Special Communications

8

Design in Print and on the Web

In today's consumer-oriented, message-dense society, people are inundated with advertisements, solicitations, entertainment, news reports, and all other manner of electronic and print documents. In this environment, people tend to read selectively, focusing only on documents that are interesting, inviting, and clear.

This is where **document design** comes in. By using headings, itemized lists, graphics, white space, effective layouts, and special typefaces, you can increase the chances that people will read your writing. These design elements can also help you emphasize the most important parts of your writing.

8a Follow the three basic design principles

Adhering to the three basic principles of graphic design will make your documents more meaningful and more readable. These principles, which we will refer to as "the three C's," are clustering, contrasting, and connecting.

❶ Clustering: grouping closely related items

Ideas or concepts that are closely related in meaning or communicative value should be clustered together visually. Instead of listing these similar concepts separately, consider how you can group them on the page for greater visual impact.

❷ Contrasting: highlighting differences

A second way of using design to make documents more meaningful and readable is to create visual contrasts that mirror important differences in content. Using variety in type size and font makes it immediately clear to the reader that elements of a document differ in content and purpose.

❸ Connecting: relating every part to some other part

The third way of employing design to make text more coherent is to repeat important graphical or typographical elements—that is, visually connect different parts of a document so that no single element is left stranded. These connections should not be made haphazardly but rather in a way that underscores connections in meaning, value, or purpose.

8b   Use formatting tools

Formatting is another powerful way of using visual representation to make a document easier to read and more emphatic in its message. Formatting can be done for decorative reasons only, but it is more effective if it also helps readers understand the text. Today's word-processing programs provide all the formatting tools you are likely to need, from boldface type to hanging indents.

❶ Headings

Headings (and subheadings and titles) draw attention, mark off parts of a text, and give the reader a quick sense of what those parts are about. Headings are especially beneficial for readers who only skim a text instead of reading it closely. Headings should give the reader an idea of what the paper, section, or illustration is about. They should be no longer than four or five words.

❷ Itemized lists

Itemized lists are a powerful form of visual clustering, as they show how several things form a closely related set. There are two main types of list formats. A *numbered list* or *lettered list* has ordered numbers or letters, suggesting either a ranking of the items or a stepwise procedure. A *bulleted list*, which uses bullets (•), diamonds (♦), dashes (—), or some other symbol, is useful for an unordered set of items.

❸ Indentation and spacing

In academic papers, the first line of each paragraph is customarily indented five spaces or one-half inch. With a word processor, you can set this indentation automatically, using either the ruler or the PARAGRAPH feature on the FORMAT menu. Quotations longer than four lines of prose or three lines of poetry are set off as a block, with each line indented ten spaces (see 21d-2).

❹ Margins

For academic papers, the standard margin is one inch all around, to give the instructor space in which to write comments. These are also the default margins used by most word-processing programs. Word processors are normally set to *left-justify* your text—that is, start lines at the left margin and leave the right margin ragged, thus avoiding the need to hyphenate at the end of a line. Academic papers are usually written with left justification.

❺ Frames and boxes

An effective way to highlight a paragraph, graphic, or other part of a document is by putting a rectangular frame or box around it. Frames and boxes are especially useful for summarizing main points or procedural steps, because they simultaneously cluster these points or steps and set them off, through contrast, from the rest of the text.

❻ Columns

Putting text into columns is a useful way of clustering information in documents such as brochures, newsletters, résumés, and Web pages. There are basically two kinds of columns: newspaper and tabular. In *newspaper columns*, the text starts on the left, flows down the first column, and then continues at the top of the next column to the right. Newspaper columns are created with the COLUMNS feature on the FORMAT menu. *Tabular columns* consist of independent texts side by side; they are created by using the TABLE feature on a word processor.

❼ Typography

Typography refers to all the features associated with individual letters, numbers, and other symbols: font type, font style, font size, color, and case.

Font type refers to the distinctive design of the typeface; some of the most common font types are `Courier`, Times New Roman, Garamond, and Arial. Font types that have little extra lines (*serifs*) at the ends of the letter strokes are called *serif fonts. Sans serif* (literally, "without serif") *fonts* lack such extra lines.

Font style (or *font weight*) refers to the particular variant of a single typeface: regular, *italic*, **bold**, or ***bold italic***. Italic, bold, and bold italic typefaces can all be used for emphasis, but they have other uses as well.

The standard *font size* range for academic papers is 10 to 12 points, with section headings often set in 14-point type and the title of the paper in 20- or even 24-point type. More specialized bulletins or reports may use a wider range of heading sizes and styles.

Color is another option that has become available with the widespread use of computers. Like bold and italic type, however, color should be used sparingly—and systematically.

One other typographical variable is *case*. Academic writers normally use the standard combination of lowercase (small) and uppercase (capital) letters, except for acronyms and other abbreviations.

❽ Page numbering

In a multipage document, it is a good idea to number the pages. Consult your word processor's documentation on how to operate the PAGE NUMBERING feature.

8c   Use graphics

Graphics include tables, line graphs, bar graphs, pie charts, clip art, photographs, cartoons, drawings, maps, and other forms of visual art.

❶ Tables

Tables are the best type of graphic for presenting a lot of data in compressed form. Current word-processing programs offer a variety of table formats to choose from. Just click on TABLE and explore the options your program gives you.

❷ Line graphs

Line graphs generally do not contain as much data as tables do. But they can make data more understandable and are especially effective for showing changes over time. If a graph has more than one line, be sure to distinguish the various lines clearly (for example, by having one solid, another dotted, and a third dashed). Do not use more than three lines in a graph, as too many lines will produce a cluttered effect.

❸ Bar graphs

Bar graphs emphasize discrete points rather than continuity, but they can also show changes over time, sometimes more dramatically than line graphs.

http://writing.colostate.edu/
Click "designing documents" for an excellent guide to using illustrations, graphics, tables, and figures in document design.

❹ Pie charts

Pie charts are effective in showing how a fixed quantity of something is divided into fractions. Generally, the entire "pie" should represent 100 percent.

❺ Clip art

http://www.clip-art.com
A great list of links to free graphics, icons, and other images on the Web

Clip art, or ready-made images, can add a decorative touch to a document. Do not get carried away, though; too much of a good thing may only distract or annoy readers. Be especially cautious about using clip art in academic papers.

❻ Photographs, cartoons, drawings, and maps

The advent of graphical scanners and Internet downloading has made it easy to incorporate photographs and other images (such as cartoons, drawings, and maps) into documents. But remember that you cannot use copyrighted materials, such as cartoons or photographs created by someone else, without permission.

8d Designing for the Web: Generate a basic design

Writing for the Web is not all that different from writing for other purposes. The basic principles outlined in Part 1 of this handbook still apply. Web documents differ from print documents in two important ways: they tend to include more graphics than print documents do, and they are **hypertextual** (that is, they have electronic links).

When a Web page is well designed, the author's message is successfully conveyed to readers, and the look and content of the page match the purposes of the author. Effectively designed Web sites thus make good use of both graphics and hypertext.

http://www.w3.org/Provider/Style/
A hypertextually organized manual on Web design from the creator of the World Wide Web, Tim Berners-Lee

WebLink

❶ Using visuals effectively

In print media, the printed words convey most of the text's meaning. But even printed texts contain other meaningful visual cues in addition to the words themselves—for example, by using boldface type for chapter titles, we also convey meaning. When Web authors consider document design, formatting, and graphics, they make decisions similar to those made by writers of print documents. However, the role of visual features in conveying meaning is greater in Web documents than in print documents.

❷ Using hypertext effectively

Hypertext goes a logical step beyond print by allowing busy readers to choose among short chunks of text on specific topics, deciding what to read and what to ignore. Hypertext is text that is broken down into discrete pieces, which are then connected through electronic links.

❸ Basic design elements

As you think about your Web site, you will need to consider whether to use some basic design elements to structure the Web pages, such as tables, frames, and style sheets. Depending on your site's purpose and the needs of your audience, you can select among these design options.

Using Tables   Tables are used by Web page authors to control page layout so that text and graphics appear on the page where they'd like them to appear. When using tables, you can decide on the number of columns and rows that will be used on each page and what data will "fill" cells formed by the intersection of those columns and rows.

Using Frames   Frames are used in a similar way as tables to organize the text and graphics on a Web site. They differ from tables, though, in their ability to show in the browser window multiple files displayed in different portions of the frame. The frame itself consistently appears on the page, but different Web pages may be displayed within the frame windows.

Using Style Sheets   Style sheets provide another sophisticated way to format your Web pages. Style sheets for the Web work in much the same way as style sheets for word-processing programs. They allow you to set default elements such as fonts and colors that will then be applied uniformly to your document.

8e   Constructing Web pages

Once you have an overall plan for your Web site, you can begin to compose your Web pages. The text of a Web site—what it "says" to the reader—is as important as how it looks; Web pages communicate through both text and graphics.

There are several methods by which to compose your Web pages—or you may use a combination of these methods.

❶ Use an HTML editor or composer, software that is designed to help with writing Web pages.

Some commonly used commercial HTML editors include *Macromedia Dreamweaver, Adobe PageMill,* and *Microsoft Front Page*. There are also HTML editors available in freeware versions that can be downloaded from the Internet (e.g., *HomeSite*).

❷ Use a translator program that changes a word-processing or database file into a Web file.

Newer versions of *Microsoft Word, WordPerfect, Excel,* and *PowerPoint,* for example, all include a SAVE AS HTML command, typically found in the FILE, SAVE AS menu. You choose this option when you have already written an extensive text in a word-processing program that you want to convert into a Web file.

❸ Use a text-editing or word-processing program (e.g., *Windows NotePad* or *Microsoft Word*), and enter the HTML code by hand.

This is the most difficult and most time-consuming method for composing Web pages. However, despite the help of the sophisticated editors and composers available today, sometimes it is still necessary to insert HTML codes by hand in order to achieve exactly the result you desire.

9   Writing for Different Purposes

In college and on the job, much of the writing you do will be "on demand"—that is, you will have a limited time in which to complete it. In college, such writing often takes the form of a timed essay exam or an in-class writing assignment. In the workplace, you may be writing a letter or an email document or preparing an oral presentation. Each of these formats requires some adjustment of your writing style.

9a   Write concise and professional business letters

Business letters are typically addressed to a specific person, but they may be circulated to other readers as well. You should make the purpose of your letter clear at the outset, and you should anticipate the possibility that someone other than the addressee (an assistant, for example) might read it. Be sure to

http://writing.colostate.edu/
click on "Business writing" for
a great guide to writing
business letters

provide whatever background information these readers might need. Be clear and concise (see Chapter 16), and try to strike a friendly, courteous, and professional tone (see 18c).

9b Write specifically tailored letters of application

A letter of application has the same general format as a business letter. It should be brief (no more than one page). The first paragraph should state clearly what position you are applying for. The next paragraph or two should describe your primary credentials for the position. The closing paragraph should express your desire for an interview and give the reader information about your availability.

9c Write appropriately packed résumés

A résumé is a concise summary of an individual's accomplishments, skills, experience, and personal interests. It is more complete and inclusive than a letter of application.

   A résumé should be densely packed with appropriate information. Most résumés use five standard categories of information: (1) Position Desired or Objective, (2) Education, (3) Experience or Employment, (4) Related Activities, and (5) References, in that order.

❶ Formatting a traditional résumé

A traditional résumé should be pleasing to the eye. Use suitable margins (about one inch all around), and use white space to set off the major categories and groupings. Use boldface type for your name and for major headings and subheadings. Using active-voice verbs will give you a dynamic image.

❷ Formatting a scannable résumé

Many companies are now using computer technology to create résumé data banks that can be computer-scanned for keywords. Take advantage of this technology by putting keyword self-descriptors such as *retail sales* and *management experience* in a separate section at the beginning of your résumé.

Computer scanners are not always reliable when it comes to distinguishing letters, numbers, and other marks on paper, so avoid anything fancy. Start every line at the left margin; do not use columns. Use light-colored, standard-size paper, a conventional typeface, and 10- to 14-point font sizes. Do not use italics, underlining, color, lines, graphics, or boxes. Print out the résumé on a high-quality printer. Do not fold or staple the résumé.

❸ Formatting an electronic résumé

Many companies solicit résumés via email or the Internet. In such cases, you should format your résumé so that it conforms to the company's specifications. This usually means (1) using a simplified layout with a prominent key-words section, like that of the scannable résumé discussed in 9d-2, and (2) putting the document in ASCII, Text Only, or Simple Text format. Rather than sending the résumé as an attached file, most companies prefer that you embed it in the email message you send in response to the company's solicitation, placing the résumé after the cover letter.

9d Practice good email etiquette

Electronic mail (email) is now widely used in most corporate and academic settings. Learning the special rules of the Internet, nicknamed **netiquette**, enables you to use this medium to best effect.

Behaviors that are not acceptable in other settings, such as verbal or sexual harassment, will not be tolerated in electronic

http://www.albion.com/netiquette/
A great netiquette homepage

WebLink

communications. Furthermore, it is not appropriate to use your classmates' or employer's email addresses for chain letters, advertising, or other similar purposes. Nor is it appropriate to use those addresses to ask someone out on a date. Also, be sensitive about "flaming"—writing angry or abusive messages. If you are flamed, do not reply in kind. Either ignore the message or respond calmly.

9e   Use file attachments

Many email systems allow you to attach files or documents to your messages. Check your mailing system for an ATTACHMENT option. Using attachments is a convenient way to send your work to a classmate for peer review or to an employer if you are away from the office. One of the advantages of using attachments over the copy-and-paste method of incorporating text into an email message is that much of your word-processing format can be preserved.

9f   Use instant messaging

Another feature of email communication is called **instant messaging**, which allows you to create a circle of email friends, classmates, or colleagues whom you have identified to your service provider (e.g., *AOL* or *MSN*). The instant messaging service will notify you whenever someone on your email group list is also online so that you can begin a "chat" session with that person via the network, should you desire to do so. (You will not be added to someone's instant messaging circle without your prior approval.)

9g   Prepare thoroughly for oral presentations

In many careers, the ability to communicate orally is just as important as the ability to write well. The basic principle to keep in mind in preparing any kind of oral presentation is this: *all listeners have a limited attention span*; you cannot expect them to follow closely everything you say. Their attention will probably wander from time to time, even if your presentation is only ten minutes long. So if you want to make sure your listeners will come away from your talk with your main points clear in their minds, you must organize your presentation in such a way that these main points stand out:

1. Limit your topic to what your audience needs to know; don't digress.

2. Determine you primary purpose.

3. Select effective supporting information, either data or evidence that will support your main point.

4. Choose an appropriate organization for your material, just as you would for a written paper.

5. Prepare an outline, including the main points and main supporting points only.

6. Select appropriate visual aids.

7. Prepare a suitable introduction so that your audience will be interested in what you have to say.

8. Prepare a closing summary that reemphasizis your main points.

9h   Pick your visual aids carefully

Visual aids are of great help in giving an oral presentation. First, they serve as "cue cards," reminding you of all your important points and allowing you to stay on track without reading from a manuscript or from notes. Second, visual aids have tremendous power as attention-getters. Studies have shown that people remember the visual parts of speeches far better than they do the verbal parts. Finally, visual aids can help clarify your message.

Pick your visual aids carefully. Here are the basic options:

- *PowerPoint* projection
- Overhead transparencies
- Chalkboard
- Flip charts or posters
- Handouts
- Three-dimensional objects

Each of these technologies has its own strengths and weaknesses and should be evaluated with the following questions in mind: Is it easy to prepare? Can it be altered easily during the presentation? Will it allow you to control the audience's attention—or will it distract attention from what you're saying? Will it let you present at an appropriate speed? How much information can it convey? How large an audience can you use it with? How reliable is it—does it depend on electronic equipment? Can the audience keep it for future reference? How well does it work as a "cue card"?

9i   Practice, practice, practice

Nothing is more helpful to the ultimate success of an oral presentation than practice. Not even the best of speakers can give a totally effective presentation without practicing it first. Practice allows you to spot the flaws in a presentation and correct them. It enables you to work on making smooth transitions instead of awkward stops and starts. Practice gives you an idea of how long your presentation will take, allowing you to make adjustments so that you can ultimately deliver it at a comfortable tempo. All of these benefits promote greater self-confidence, which will give you a more emphatic, convincing, and effective style of delivery.

9j   Speak with enthusiasm and focus

As the time draws near for delivering your oral presentation, you will experience what all speakers do—nervousness. One key to an effective delivery is to convert your nervousness into the kind of energy that injects liveliness, enthusiasm, and animation into your speech.

How can you control your nervousness? First of all, make sure you're properly prepared for your talk. This means getting all your visual aids and notes organized and making sure you're properly dressed and groomed. Your personal appearance is one of the most powerful "visual aids" you have. If you know you're looking your best, it will give you a boost in confidence.

Second, as you are about to start your presentation, look for an opportunity to say something off the cuff. For example, you could acknowledge the occasion or you could share a spontaneous bit of humor. Don't feel you have to tell a prepared joke or story. If you're good at joketelling or storytelling, fine, but don't force it.

Finally, as you are actually giving your presentation, *concentrate your full attention on what you want to say*. Stick to your outline, and make sure you cover all your main supporting points. Convince your listeners that the topic is important, and be enthusiastic about it. Show each of your visual aids long enough for the audience to understand and appreciate it, and then move on to the next one. Keep up the pace; don't dally.

Encourage questions from the audience, but don't let questions disrupt your presentation. Above all, do not show any antagonism toward a questioner. Any hint of annoyance on your part will make your entire audience feel uncomfortable, and people may hold it against you, even if the questioner is unfair or unpleasant.

9k   Use *PowerPoint*

Presentation software such as *PowerPoint* is becoming more and more common because it has almost all the benefits of overhead transparencies plus some special advantages: it projects color better than overhead transparencies; it can include animation, video, and sound; and it can be converted into HTML and put on a Web site for later reference. Also, it has a wizard and templates to guide you through the process of putting together a presentation. Although the templates are business-oriented, some of them can be adapted to academic presentations as well.

As with overhead transparencies, *PowerPoint* slides should be neatly formatted, easily readable, and not too cluttered with information. If the presentation is in a darkened room, the slides should have a light background; in a well-lit room, they should have a darker background. Any visual images or background sound should be relevant to the theme of the presentation.

http://www.canberra.edu.au/studyskills/learning/oral
Helpful tips for preparing and delivering an oral presentation, with advice on the use of *PowerPoint*.

WebLink

Common Grammar Problems

10 Sentence Structure

Improving your grammar and writing style will allow you to express your thoughts more precisely and make your writing more readable and interesting. To improve your style, you will need to know the basic elements of sentence structure. This chapter provides that information.

10a Learn to identify parts of speech

In writing a sentence, you put words together in certain combinations. These combinations depend, in part, on the different kinds of words, or parts of speech, you use: nouns, pronouns, verbs, adjectives, adverbs, prepositions, conjunctions, and interjections.

❶ Nouns

A **noun** (n) is the name of a person, place, thing, quality, idea, or action. Some examples of nouns are

Picasso	Mexico	printer
honesty	democracy	stamp collecting

Nouns are often preceded by *a, an,* or *the*; these words are known as **articles**. Use *a* before nouns beginning with a consonant sound; use *an* before nouns beginning with a vowel sound: *a* printer, *an* insult.

Common nouns refer to general persons, places, things, concepts, or qualities: *city, generosity*.

Proper nouns, always capitalized, name particular persons, places, institutions, organizations, months, and days: *Buddhism, Monday*.

Concrete nouns refer to things that can be sensed through sight, hearing, touch, taste, or smell: *bookshelf, thunder*.

Abstract nouns refer to ideas, emotions, qualities, or other intangible concepts: *sadness, truth*.

Count nouns name things that can be counted and thus can have a plural form: *violin, violins; goose, geese*.

Noncount nouns, or mass nouns, name things that typically are not counted in English and thus cannot be made plural: *water, health*.

Collective nouns name groups; they are plural in sense but singular in form: *committee, crowd*.

❷ Pronouns

Pronouns (pron), such as *she, they*, and *it*, are words that substitute for nouns. The noun a pronoun substitutes for is called the **antecedent** of the pronoun. The noun antecedent often precedes the pronoun in a sentence:

Lucinda said *she* was not feeling well.

Sometimes the noun antedecent follows the pronoun:

Saying *she* was not feeling well, *Lucinda* left the room.

Pronouns can be singular or plural, and their case form can vary, depending on how they are used in a sentence. (See Chapter 11 for a discussion of pronoun case and pronoun-antecedent agreement.)

❸ Verbs

A **verb** (v) is a word that expresses an action (*swim, read*) or a state of being (*is, seemed*). Main verbs are often accompanied by **auxiliary verbs** (also called helping verbs), which include forms of the verbs *be, have*, and *do*, and/or by **modal verbs**, such as *may, might, can, could, will, would, shall, should*, and *must*. Auxiliary and modal verbs are critical parts of special verb forms that express questions, future tenses, past tenses, and various degrees of doubt about or qualification of the main verb's action. (See Chapter 11 for more on verbs.)

Transitive verbs (vt) transfer action from an agent (usually the subject of the sentence) to an object or recipient (usually the direct object of the sentence): "Michael *fumbled* the ball." **Intransitive verbs** (vi) may express action, but they do not transfer it to an object or recipient: "The bridge *collapsed*."

Verbs also have an active form, called the **active voice** ("He *committed* the crime"), as well as a passive form, called the **passive voice**, consisting of a form of the verb *be* and a past participle ("A crime *was committed*"). Verbs may take alternative forms for different **moods**. In the **indicative mood**, they make assertions, state opinions, and ask questions (as in this sentence). In the **subjunctive mood**, they use past-tense forms to express unreal conditions or wishes: "I wish I *were* in Hawaii." In the **imperative mood**, they use the base form to issue a command: "Don't *do* that again!"

❹ Verbals

A **verbal** is a verb form that functions in a sentence as a noun, an adverb, or an adjective. There are three types of verbals: participles, gerunds, and infinitives.

Participles are words such as *sweeping* and *swept*, the present and past participles of a verb (*sweep*) that function as adjectives and can modify nouns or pronouns: "Beware of *sweeping* generalizations." "Keep floors *swept*."

Gerunds are verb forms that end in *ing* and function as nouns: "*Sweeping* is something I do not enjoy."

An **infinitive** is the base form of a verb, often preceded by *to* (*to read*, *to fly*). Infinitives can function as nouns, adjectives, or adverbs: "*To quit* would be a mistake." "Her desire *to quit* is understandable."

❺ Adjectives

An **adjective** (adj) is a word that modifies a noun or pronoun by qualifying or describing it. In English, the adjective usually precedes the noun it modifies (an *old* tree, the *other* day). In sentences such as "The program was *challenging*," the adjective falls on the other side of a verb linking it to the noun it modifies. An adjective used in this way is called a **predicate adjective**.

Many adjectives have comparative and superlative forms created by the addition of *-er* and *-est* (*small*, *smaller*, *smallest*). (See Chapter 11.) Many other adjectives have the same form as the present or past participle of a verb (a *roaring* lion, a *deserted* island).

❻ Adverbs

An **adverb** (adv) modifies a verb, an adjective, another adverb, or an entire clause or sentence. Adverbs usually answer one of the following questions: When? Where? How? How often? To what extent?

> The mayor lives *alone* in a downtown apartment. [*Alone* modifies the verb *lives*.]

> She has a *very* busy schedule. [*Very* modifies the adjective *busy*.]

Conjunctive adverbs, such as *however, thus,* and *consequently,* modify an entire sentence or clause while linking it to the preceding sentence or clause. (See Chapter 11.)

❼ Prepositions

A **preposition** (prep) is a word such as *in, on, of, for,* or *by* that comes before a noun or pronoun and its modifiers to form a **prepositional phrase** (*in the water, off the deep end*). The noun or pronoun in such phrases (*water, end*) is called the **object of the preposition**. Prepositions also occur in multiword combinations: *according to, along with, because of,* and *with respect to.* Prepositions can be linked to certain verbs to form **phrasal verbs**, such as *do without, put up with,* and *look over.* In phrasal verbs, the preposition is called a **particle**.

❽ Conjunctions

A **conjunction** (conj) joins two sentences, clauses, phrases, or words. The relationship between the two parts may be an equal, or coordinate, one; it may be an unequal, or subordinate, one.

Coordinating conjunctions (*and, but, or, nor, yet, so, for*) connect sentences, clauses, phrases, or words that are parallel in meaning and grammatical structure. **Correlative conjunctions** (*both/and, neither/nor, either/or, not/but, whether/or, not only/but also*) are pairs of conjunctions that give extra emphasis to the two parts of a coordinated construction. **Subordinating conjunctions** introduce dependent clauses and connect them to main clauses. Some common subordinating conjunctions are *although, because, if, since, unless,* and *while.*

⑨ Interjections

An **interjection** is a short utterance like *wow!* or *ouch!* that expresses an emotional response. Interjections usually stand alone and are punctuated with an exclamation point.

10b Learn to identify basic sentence patterns

Sentences are the basic units for expressing assertions, questions, commands, wishes, and exclamations. All grammatically complete sentences have a subject and a predicate. In a sentence fragment, one of these elements may be missing. (See Chapter 12 for more on fragments.)

❶ Sentence subjects

The **subject** (sub) of a sentence is a noun, a pronoun, or a noun phrase that identifies what the sentence is about. Usually it directly precedes the main verb.

You probably have a pointing device (PD) connected to your computer.

Many PDs have ergonomic features.

The **simple subject** is always a noun or pronoun. In the sample sentence, the simple subject is *you*. The complete subject is the simple subject plus all its modifiers; the **complete subjects** are italicized in the sample sentences. Some sentences have a **compound subject** including two or more simple subjects: "*Tips and techniques* can be found in the HELP menu." In imperative sentences, which express a command or a request, the subject is understood to be *you*, even though it is not usually stated: "[You] Wake up!" The subject of a sentence always agrees in number with the main verb. That is, a singular subject takes a singular verb, and a plural subject takes a plural verb: "Many *PDs have*." Subject-verb agreement is discussed further in Chapter 13.

WebLink

http://owl.english.purdue.edu/
handouts/grammar/index.html
Comprehensive coverage of
parts of speech and sentence
construction

❷ Predicates

The **predicate** is the part of a sentence that contains the verb and makes a statement about the subject. The **simple predicate** is the verb plus any auxiliary (helping) verbs: "With a Web browser, you *can locate* information efficiently." The **complete predicate** consists of the simple predicate plus any objects, complements, or adverbial modifiers: "The World Wide Web *offers information, media, and software*." A **compound predicate** has two or more verbs that have the same subject: "A Web page *informs and entertains*."

A **direct object** (DO) is a noun, a pronoun, or a noun phrase that completes the action of a transitive verb (see 10b-3)—one that is capable of transmitting action. In this sentence, *information* is the direct object of the verb *locate*:

Sub   V   DO
You can locate *information*.

An **indirect object** (IO) is a noun, a pronoun, or a noun phrase that is affected indirectly by the action of a verb. It usually refers to the recipient or beneficiary of the action described by the verb and the direct object.

Sub   V   IO   DO
The teacher told *us* a story.

Most indirect objects can be presented instead as the object of the preposition *to* or *for*:

The teacher told *us* a story.   OR   The teacher told a story *to us*.

An **object complement** (OC) is a noun, a noun phrase, an adjective, or an adjective phrase that elaborates on or describes the direct object.

Sub   V   DO   OC
The news made us *depressed*.

A **subject complement** (SC) is a noun, a noun phrase, an adjective, or an adjective phrase that follows a linking verb (such as *is, was,* or *seems*) and elaborates on the subject:

Sub   LV SC   Sub LV   SC
Laurie is *happy*. She is *the new head of the task force*.

❸ Basic sentence patterns

The complete predicate is usually structured according to one of five basic patterns.

Pattern 1: A sentence may have an intransitive verb and no object.

```
        Pred
      ┌────┐
Sub    V
```

Time flies.

Pattern 2: A sentence may have a transitive verb with a direct object.

```
          Pred
      ┌──────────┐
Sub    VT    DO
```

Time heals all wounds.

Pattern 3: A sentence may have a transitive verb with a direct object and an indirect object.

```
                  Pred
          ┌─────────────────┐
    Sub    VT   IO    DO
```

Free time gave us an opportunity.

Pattern 4: A sentence may have a transitive verb with a direct object and an object complement.

```
                Pred
          ┌──────────────┐
    Sub    VT   DO   OC
```

Time pressures made us tense.

Pattern 5: A sentence may use a linking verb, which connects the subject to a subject complement, indicating a condition, quality, or state of being.

```
        Pred
      ┌──────┐
Sub   LV   SC
```

Time is precious.

10c Vary your sentence types

Good writers vary the types of sentences they use in order to make their writing more interesting. The two main categories of sentence types are functional and structural.

❶ Functional classifications

Sentences can differ functionally, or rhetorically, according to their role. A **declarative sentence**, for example, makes a direct assertion about something: "Our political system is heavily influenced by corporate interests." An **interrogative sentence** asks a question and ends with a question mark: "Have you ever traveled overseas?" An **imperative sentence** makes a request, gives a command, or offers advice. Although it is always addressed to *you*, the pronoun is usually omitted: "Use the TOOLBAR buttons to align or indent text." An **exclamatory sentence** expresses strong emotion and ends with an exclamation point: "We're finally connected!"

❷ Structural classifications

Sentences can also differ according to their overall grammatical construction. A **simple sentence** has a single independent clause and no dependent clauses. Although a simple sentence has only one clause, it may have many phrases and thus be quite long.

> I walk.

> The high plateau of western Bolivia, called the *altiplano*, is one of the world's highest-elevation populated regions, with several towns located more than 12,000 feet above sea level.

A **compound sentence** has two or more independent clauses and no dependent clauses. A compound sentence is created when two or more independent clauses are connected with a comma and a coordinating conjunction (*and, or, but, nor, for, so, yet*), with a semicolon and a conjunctive adverb (*therefore, however, otherwise, indeed*), with a semicolon alone, or with a correlative conjunction (*either/or, neither/nor, both/and, not only/but also*).

Ind cl   Ind cl

An eagle once flew past our house, *but* I got only a brief glimpse of it.

A **complex sentence** contains one independent clause and one or more dependent clauses.

Dep cl   Ind cl

Although Alaska is a huge state, it has relatively few people.

11 Pronouns, Verbs, Adjectives, and Adverbs

Now that you have learned to identify different parts of speech, you need to learn how to use them correctly. This chapter will help you avoid common usage problems with pronouns, verbs, adjectives, and adverbs.

PRONOUNS

Sometimes using pronouns in place of nouns can make writing more concise and readable. But pronouns can be confusing to readers if they are not used correctly.

11a Make pronouns agree with their antecedents

A **pronoun** substitutes for a noun (or noun equivalent), which is called the **antecedent** of the pronoun (10a-2). Singular pronouns should have singular antecedents; plural pronouns should have plural antecedents.

Antecedent   Pronoun

Bad luck can happen to anyone, and *it* can happen at any time.

In this sentence, *bad luck* and *it* are both singular; therefore, they agree in *number*. They also agree in gender because *bad luck* is neuter (neither masculine nor feminine) and *it* can serve as a pronoun for neuter antecedents.

Here are some rules on pronoun-antecedent agreement.

1. *A compound antecedent is usually is plural and so requires a plural pronoun.* A **compound antecedent** is a noun phrase containing two or more terms joined by *and*.

   Mr. and Mrs. Kwan are here for *their* appointment.

2. *With disjunctive antecedents, the pronoun should agree in number and gender with the nearest part.* A **disjunctive antecedent** is a noun phrase consisting of two or more terms joined by *or* or *nor*. When a disjunctive antecedent contains both a singular and a plural part, this rule works well if the singular noun precedes the plural one.

   http://ccc.commnet.edu/grammar/pronouns1.htm
   A fun guide to pronoun agreement, with quizzes and exercises

   Either Tamara Wilson or *the Changs* will bring *their* barbeque set to the next picnic.

   If the plural noun precedes the singular one, however, following the rule usually leads to an awkward-sounding sentence:

   Either the Changs or *Tamara Wilson* will bring *her* barbeque set to the next picnic.

   In such cases, it is best to reword the sentence so as to either get rid of the pronoun or put the singular noun before the plural one.

3. *As an antecedent, a collective noun can be either singular or plural, depending on its sense.* Both of these sentences are correct:

   The jury took only two hours to reach *its* verdict.

   The jury took only two hours to reach *their* verdict.

The first sentence emphasizes the singularity of the jury as a body, while the second puts more emphasis on the jury as a group of individuals.

4. *Pronouns must agree with antecedents that are indefinite pronouns.* Most indefinite pronouns (such as *everybody*, *anyone*, and *each*) are singular. When an indefinite pronoun serves as the antecedent for another pronoun, that pronoun should also be singular.

Everything was in *its* place.

Each of the women had *her* reasons for opposing the plan.

Some indefinite pronouns (*some, all, more*) can have either a singular or a plural sense. When one of these indefinite pronouns is used as the antecedent for another pronoun, the other pronoun can be either singular or plural, depending on the sense of the sentence.

Some of the *news* was as bad as we thought *it* would be.

Some of the team's *players* have lost *their* motivation.

5. *Sexist use of generic pronouns should be avoided.* In the past, the male pronouns *he, him,* and *his* were often used in generic statements referring to both sexes, as in this sentence: "A doctor should listen carefully to *his* patients." But this practice is clearly sexist, as it favors one gender over the other. Three ways to avoid such sexist pronoun usage are (1) making the pronoun and its antecedent plural, (2) rewording the sentence, and (3) using an occasional disjunctive pronoun such as *he or she*.

11b   Refer to a specific noun antecedent

Pronouns (such as *she, it*, and *his*) work best when they clearly refer to a particular noun (the antecedent).

The new hockey player knew what *his* position would be.

❶ Avoiding generalized *they* or *you* or implied antecedents

In casual speech, people often use pronouns in vague ways, without explicit antecedents ("*They* say that television is dulling our brains"). In formal writing, however, such vagueness can sabotage meaning and must be avoided.

VAGUE *THEY* REVISED

Some people

~~They~~ say that television is dulling our brains.

Similarly, avoid using the pronoun *you* unless you are addressing the reader directly.

VAGUE *YOU* REVISED

One never knows

~~You never know~~ when calamity will strike.

Pronouns should refer to specific antecedents, not implied ones.

❷ Clarifying references with more than one possible antecedent

Writers sometimes get into trouble by using a pronoun that could refer to more than one noun. Usually it is necessary to rewrite the sentence so that the antecedent is named, whether or not it has been mentioned previously in the sentence.

VAGUE REFERENCE REVISED

Fred

Neither Bill nor Fred knew what ~~he~~ should do.

OR

their friend

Neither Bill nor Fred knew what ~~he~~ should do.

If *he* refers either to Fred or to a mutual friend mentioned in a previous sentence, it is important to say so.

11c Avoid vague use of *this*, *that*, *which*, and *it*

The pronouns *this, that, which,* and *it* may be used with care to refer broadly to an entire statement:

> According to the linguistic school currently on top, human beings are all born with a genetic endowment for recognizing and formulating language. *This*

must mean that we possess genes for all kinds of information, with strands of special, peculiarly human DNA for the discernment of meaning in syntax.

—Lewis Thomas, *Lives of a Cell*

In this excerpt, the word *this* leading off the second sentence refers clearly to the main clause of the first sentence ("human beings . . . language").

In many cases, though, using pronouns for broad reference may confuse the reader. What does *it* refer to in the following paragraph?

Watching <u>Monday night football</u> on ESPN has become a ritual for countless American sports lovers. <u>It</u> is symbolic of contemporary American life.

It could refer to (1) <u>Monday night football</u>, (2) watching <u>Monday night football</u>, or (3) the ritual of watching <u>Monday night football</u>. One way to resolve this ambiguity is to replace the pronoun with a full noun phrase:

VAGUE REFERENCE REVISED

Watching <u>Monday night football</u> on ESPN has become a ritual for

This ritual

countless American sports lovers. ~~It~~ is symbolic of contemporary

American life.

11d   Be consistent with use of *that* and *which*

The relative pronoun *that* is used only with essential (restrictive) relative clauses—clauses that are essential to identify the nouns they modify:

ESSENTIAL CLAUSE

First prize went to the long-haired collie *that came all the way from Hartford.*

[There were other long-haired collies in the competition.]

Although many people prefer using *which* only for nonessential relative clauses, it can be used either with essential relative clauses or with nonessential (nonrestrictive) relative clauses—clauses that merely add extra information:

NONESSENTIAL CLAUSE

First prize went to the long-haired collie, *which came all the way from Hartford.*

[It was the only long-haired collie in the competition.]

ESSENTIAL CLAUSE

> First prize went to the long-haired collie *which came all the way from Hartford.*
>
> [There were other long-haired collies in the competition.]

Use *I, he, she, we, them,* or *who* for sentence or clause subjects

The **subjective case** (*I, you, he, she, it, we, they, who, whoever*) is required for all pronouns used as subjects, including pronouns that are paired with a noun to form a compound subject or to rename the noun (see 11g).

> *She* and Octavio are good friends. [Sentence subject]

> It seems that only Harrison and *I* were not invited. [Clause subject]

In predicate nominative constructions, the verb *be* is used to set up an "equation" between a noun subject or a pronoun subject such as *it, that, this* and a personal pronoun such as *he, she, it,* or *they.*

>   *she.*
> "Hello, is Carol there?" "Yes, this is ~~her~~."

>   *he*   *I*
> Who will be the lead actor— ~~him~~ or ~~me~~?

Use *me, him, her, us, then,* or *whom* for sentence or clause objects

The **objective case** (*me, you, him, her, it, us, them, whom, whomever*) is required for all pronouns used as objects, indirect objects, and objects of prepositions, including any pronoun paired with a noun or another pronoun to form a compound object.

> The boss invited Janice and *him* to lunch. [Pronoun as indirect object]

> Just between *you* and *me,* don't you think Marty's been a little out of line lately? [Pronoun as object of a preposition]

11g Test for pronouns in compound constructions by using the pronoun alone

Most problems with pronoun case arise in compound constructions, when a pronoun is paired with a noun:

> The instructor gave Natasha and [*me, I*] an extra project to do.

In such sentences, the case of the pronoun—subjective or objective—depends on its function in the sentence. If you are unsure about which case to use, the best way to find out is to try the sentence without the noun:

> The instructor gave [*me, I*] an extra project to do.

Seeing it in this form makes it easier to decide what the correct form is:

> The instructor gave Natasha and *me* an extra project to do.

A special type of pronoun-noun pairing, called an **appositive**, occurs when a pronoun is conjoined with a noun.

> *We Americans* tend to be patriotic.

> Sometimes people from other countries complain about *us Americans*.

Again, if you are unsure about which case to use in such situations, just omit the noun and see which pronoun form is correct.

> *We* tend to be patriotic.

> Sometimes people from other countries complain about *us*.

11h Choose *who* or *whom* based on how it functions in its clause

The pronouns *who, whom, whoever, whomever*, and *whose* are used in questions and modifying clauses. In questions, they are called **interrogative pronouns**; in clauses, they are called **relative pronouns**.

Who reserved this book? [Interrogative pronoun]

I'd like to find the person *who* reserved this book. [Relative pronoun]

When you ask a question and reverse normal sentence word order, choosing the correct interrogative pronoun can be puzzling. As a writer, you must decide whether the *wh-* pronoun functions as a subject or an object in the clause in which it is used.

[*Who, Whom*] are you going to invite to the wedding?

 11i   Is it *more than me* or *more than I*? Use pronouns in a comparison based on how they would function in a full clause

What is the meaning of this sentence?

Mark likes school more than me.

Technically, it means that Mark has a greater liking for school than he does for the speaker of the sentence. It does not mean that Mark has a greater liking for school than the speaker does. The latter meaning is correctly expressed with this construction:

Mark likes school more than I.

You can avoid this problem by recognizing that the second part of the comparison (the part after *than*) is an incomplete clause. The complete versions of the two sentences make the distinction clear:

Mark likes school more than [he likes] me.
Mark likes school more than I [like school].

A similar procedure can be used with *as . . . as* constructions.

VERBS

Using verbs correctly can help make writing lively and precise. This section explains some of the major aspects of verb usage: form, tense, voice, and mood. (Two other aspects, gender and number, are discussed in 11a.)

11j Learn the regular verb forms

All verbs in English, except *be*, have five basic forms or **principal parts**.

Base form	*Present tense (-s form)*	*Past tense*	*Past participle*	*Present participle*
jump	jumps	jumped	jumped	jumping
erase	erases	erased	erased	erasing
veto	vetoes	vetoed	vetoed	vetoing

Most English verbs are **regular verbs**. Their forms follow the pattern of the preceding examples: adding *-s* (or *-es*) to the base form to make the third-person singular present tense, adding *-d* (or *-ed*) to make the past tense and past participle, and adding *-ing* to the base form (and sometimes dropping the final *e*) to make the present participle.

The base form, or simple form, of a verb is the form listed in a dictionary, the form normally used with plural nouns or the pronouns *I, you, we,* or *they* in the present tense: "Hummingbirds *migrate* south in winter." "I *walk* two miles every day."

When the subject of a sentence is *he, she, it,* or some other third-person singular subject, the **present tense** of the verb has *-s* added to it: "She *visits* New York every month." "My neighbor *walks* laps around our block." Sometimes a slight change is required in the spelling of the base form (*fly/flies, veto/vetoes*).

The **past tense** of a verb is used to describe action that occurred in the past. For a regular verb, add *-d* or *-ed* to the base form to get the past tense: "Fox TV *televised* Super Bowl XL." "We *wanted* to see the game."

The **past participle** of a regular verb is similar in form to the past tense. The past participle can be used (1) with *has* or *have* in the present perfect tense, (2) with *had* in the past perfect tense, (3) with some form of *be* to create a passive-voice construction, and (4) by itself, as an adjective, to modify a noun.

We *have petitioned* the school board for a new crosswalk. [Present perfect]

Before last night's meeting, we *had talked* about going directly to the mayor. [Past perfect]

Last year, two students *were injured* trying to cross this street. [Passive voice]

The parents of the *injured* students are supporting our cause. [Adjective]

The **present participle** is created by adding *-ing* to the base form of a verb. It is used (1) with some form of *be* to indicate ongoing action (the progressive tense), (2) as a gerund, and (3) as an adjective.

Joaquin *is working* on a new project. [Progressive tense]

He enjoys *working*. [Gerund]

This is a *working* draft of my paper. [Adjective]

11k Learn common irregular verb forms

An **irregular verb** is one whose past tense and past participle do not follow the standard pattern of being created by adding *-d* or *-ed* to the base form. Common irregular verbs and their past tense and past participle forms include these:

Base form	Past tense	Past participle
be	was, were	been
go	went	gone
swim	swam	swum

11l Know how to use auxiliary verbs

An **auxiliary verb** (or **helping verb**) is one that is used with a main verb to indicate tense, mood, or voice. The most common auxiliary verbs are *be*, *have*, *will*, and *do*.

She *is finishing* her paper. [Progressive tense, indicating ongoing action]

The college *has adopted* a new honor code. [Present perfect tense, indicating past action with ongoing effects]

We *do need* to get going. [Emphasis]

My roommate *has been asked* to run for the student senate. [Passive voice, present perfect tense]

Will he *know* what's involved? [Question]

Other important helping verbs are the **modal auxiliary verbs** (*may/might, can/could, will/would, shall/should, must, ought to,* and *have to*). These verbs communicate degrees of probability, necessity, or obligation. A modal auxiliary verb is used only with the base form of another verb:

The concert *might be* sold out.

We *should get* tickets before it is too late.

Modal auxiliaries can be used with forms of *be, have,* or *do,* but not with other modal auxiliaries.

NONSTANDARD   We might *could* do that.

REVISED   We might *be able to* do that. [Verb phrase substituted]

In some cases, you can simply eliminate one of the modal auxiliaries:

NONSTANDARD   Sally *should ought to* cancel her appointment.

REVISED   Sally *should* cancel her appointment.

                 OR

                 Sally *ought* to cancel her appointment.

 11m Use transitive and intransitive verbs correctly: *sit/set, lie/lay, rise/raise*

A **transitive verb** is a verb that takes a direct object (see 10a-3). In other words, a transitive verb transfers an action from a subject to an object. The sentence "A virus damaged my hard drive" has a transitive verb (*damaged*) that transfers the action to the direct object (*hard drive*). Some typical transitive verbs are *see, hear, consult, kick, recognize,* and *mix.* Transitive verbs are usually marked in dictionaries with the abbreviation *vt* or *tr.*

An **intransitive verb** is one that does not take a direct object. Some typical intransitive verbs are *sleep, relax, die, go, fall, come,* and *walk.* Intransitive verbs are usually identified in dictionaries by the abbreviation *vi* or *intr.*

Many speakers of English confuse *sit* and *set*, *lie* and *lay*, and *rise* and *raise*. The two verbs in each of these pairs sound somewhat alike and have related meanings, but they differ as to whether they can take an object. The first member of each pair is intransitive and cannot take an object; the second member is transitive and does take an object.

INTRANSITIVE   Jorge *will sit* over there. [The verb has no object.]

TRANSITIVE   Jorge *will set* the *flowers* over there. [The verb has an object, *flowers*.]

11n   Favor active over passive voice

Voice is the characteristic of a verb that indicates whether the subject of a sentence is acting or being acted on. In the **active voice**, the subject of the sentence performs an action on a direct object (see 10b). In the **passive voice**, the subject of the sentence is acted on. Only transitive verbs can be cast in active and passive voice.

           Subject/actor   DO

ACTIVE   My friend Julie *handcrafted* this pin. [The subject acts on an object.]

          Subject   DO/actor

PASSIVE   This pin was *handcrafted* by my friend Julie. [The subject is acted on by the object following the verb.]

The passive voice consists of an appropriate form of the auxiliary verb *be* and the past participle of a main verb (see 11j). A passive-voice sentence may refer to the performer of the action in a *by* phrase following the verb. In practice, though, the *by* phrase is often omitted, which has the effect of concealing or deemphasizing the performer of the action: "This pin *was handcrafted*."

http://ccc.commnet.edu/grammar/
verbs.htm#verb
A superb resource on verbs,
including quizzes and lots of cool
graphics

In general, good writers favor the active voice over the passive voice. The active voice is more concise and more direct—and thus more vigorous—than the passive. In some cases, however, the passive voice works better than the active: "Bacterial infections are usually treated with antibiotics."

11o Use correct verb forms after *if* or *that*

The **subjunctive mood** is used for hypothetical conditions, polite requests, wishes, and other uncertain statements. A verb in the subjunctive mood often appears in dependent clauses beginning with *if* or *that*. The present subjunctive is the same as the base form of the verb. The past subjunctive is identical to the past tense of the verb. The only exception is *were*, which is used for all subjunctive uses of *be* except after verbs of requesting, requiring, or recommending, where *be* is used: "I wish I *were* an A student!" "She asked that her client *be* given probation." The past perfect subjunctive has the same form as the ordinary past perfect.

❶ Hypothetical *if* constructions

When an *if* clause expresses a contrary-to-fact or unreal condition, the verb of the clause should be in the past subjunctive or past perfect subjunctive mood. The main clause verb should include the modal auxiliary *would*, *could*, or *might*.

If I *were* you, I *would* make up my incompletes as soon as possible.
[Expresses a hypothetical future condition]

If John *had been* there, he *might* have been able to help.
[Expresses a hypothetical past condition]

Do not use *would, could,* or *might* in a hypothetical *if* clause. In contrary-to-fact sentences, modal auxiliaries such as *would* and *could* belong in the main clause, not in the conditional (subordinate) clause. Use the subjunctive in the conditional clause.

SUBJUNCTIVE FORM REVISED
        lived
If we ~~would live~~ closer to San Francisco, we would go there more often.

❷ Dependent clauses expressing a wish

In a dependent clause following the verb *wish*, use the past subjunctive for present contrary-to-fact conditions and the past perfect subjunctive for past contrary-to-fact conditions: "I wish [that] he *were* here." "I wish [that] he *had stayed*."

❸ Dependent clauses expressing a request, suggestion, or demand

Verbs like *require, demand, suggest,* and *insist* are usually followed by a dependent clause beginning with *that.* The verb in the *that* clause should be in the subjunctive mood: "The police require that all pets *be* kept on a leash." Sometimes *that* is omitted.

ADJECTIVES AND ADVERBS

Using adjectives and adverbs allows writers to add details to their work, making it more precise and colorful. But adjectives and adverbs have their proper uses, and it is important not to confuse them or use them incorrectly.

11p   Use adjectives to modify nouns

An **adjective** is a word that modifies a noun (see 10a-5). Typically, adjectives answer one of the following questions: Which? What kind? How many?

Sometimes an adjective is placed next to the noun it modifies, either directly before the noun (an *ancient* building, the *first* page) or directly after (a dream *forsaken*, his curiosity *satisfied*). Other times an adjective is separated from the noun it modifies, as in the sentence "The movie was *exciting*." In these cases, a linking verb (such as *is, was,* or *seemed*) connects the noun and its modifier to form a predicate adjective and a subject complement.

http://www.uottawa.ca/academic/arts/writcent/hypergrammar/adjective.html
A complete discussion of adjectives

WebLink

11q   Avoid overuse of nouns as modifiers

A noun can modify another noun and thus function as an adjective. Some examples are *park* bench, *soda* pop, *letter* opener, *telephone* book, *fender* bender, *tape* player, and *movie* theater.

Such noun compounding can help you save a few words—*windshield* is more concise than *shield against the wind*—but it can be confusing for readers, especially if you use more than three nouns in a row. To avoid long noun strings like *the picnic table cross brace*, use a prepositional phrase: *the cross brace under the picnic table*. Such phrasing may take a few more words, but the meaning will be clearer.

11r   Use adverbs to modify verbs, adjectives, other adverbs, and clauses

An adverb is a word that modifies a verb, an adjective, another adverb, or a clause (see 10a-6). Adverbs modify verbs by answering such questions as these: When? How? How often? Where? To what degree?

Linda *often* goes to the gym to work out.   [Modifies the verb *goes*]

They made a *very* bad mistake.   [Modifies the adjective *bad*]

The car was turned *almost* upside down.   [Modifies the adverb *upside down*]

Luckily, I was able to find a backup disk.   [Modifies the entire clause]

11s   Don't confuse *good* and *well* or *bad* and *badly*

The pairs of words *good/well* and *bad/badly* are misused by many writers who fail to recognize that *good* and *bad* are adjectives, whereas *well* and *badly* are adverbs. The sentence "Fielder runs *good* for a man his size" is ungrammatical. The correct version is

Fielder runs *well* for a man his size. [The adverb *well* modifies the verb *runs*.]

The adjective *good* is appropriate when the word being modified is a noun.

He has a *good*, long stride. [The adjective *good* modifies the noun *stride*.]

When the main verb expresses a feeling or a perception (such verbs include *look*, *appear*, *feel*, *seem*, *taste*, and *smell*), the correct modifier is an adjective complement.

> I feel *bad* about what I did. [Not *badly*; the adjective *bad* modifies the noun *I*.]
>
> This gazpacho tastes *good*. [Not *well*; the adjective *good* modifies the noun *gazpacho*.]

 11t   Use comparative and superlative forms of adjectives and adverbs correctly

Most adjectives and a few adverbs can be used to make comparisons.

> Ted works *hard*. He is *determined* to get ahead. [Positive form]
>
> Ted works *harder* than I do. He is *more determined* than I am. [Comparative forms]
>
> Ted works the *hardest* of anybody I know. He is the *most determined* person I have ever met. [Superlative forms]

When making comparisons, be accurate, complete, and logical. When comparing two items, use the comparative form. When comparing three or more items, use the superlative form.

> Of the two candidates, I like Johnson *better*.
>
> Of the three candidates, I like Johnson *best*.

Use *few*, *fewer*, or *fewest* with count nouns (such as *books*, *calories*, *flowers*, and *dollars*). Use *little*, *less*, or *least* with noncount nouns (such as *water*, *understanding*, and *progress*).

> The team has *fewer* fans than it used to have.
>
> The new package contains *less* rice.

Make sure the terms of a comparison are complete. Do not write a sentence like "This headache remedy works better." Many readers will wonder, "Better than what?" Including a *than* phrase as part of the comparison makes it clear:

> This headache remedy works better *than any other*.

11u Avoid double negatives

A **double negative** is a sentence or phrase containing two negative modifiers (typically adverbs such as *never, no, not, hardly, barely*, and *scarcely*) that carry the same meaning. Double negatives are considered nonstandard in modern English and should be avoided in formal writing and speaking.

> *any*
> The city buses do not have ~~no~~ lifts for disabled passengers.

> *can*
> The passengers ~~can't~~ hardly get on board.

12 Sentence Fragments, Comma Splices, and Run-On Sentences

Now that you have learned grammar rules about individual parts of speech, you have mastered common sentence structure. This chapter covers the problems of sentence fragments, comma splices, and run-on sentences.

SENTENCE FRAGMENTS

A fragment is a grammatically incomplete sentence. Complete sentences (1) have a complete predicate, (2) have a grammatical subject, and (3) do not begin with a subordinating conjunction or relative pronoun unless they are connected to a main clause.

12a   Make sentences grammatically complete

If you have a good style or grammar checker on your computer, it should identify most of the sentence fragments in your writing. But it will not be able to tell you how to fix them. So you will need to solve these problems on your own. (See also 10b.)

❶ Does the sentence have a complete predicate?

In standard English, all sentences must have a complete predicate—that is, a main verb plus any necessary helping verbs and complements. The main verb must be a *finite* verb, not an infinitive (*to* form) or a gerund (*-ing* form).

The second part of the following example has been incorrectly set off as a separate sentence; it does not have a finite verb and so cannot be a full sentence:

> Seven is a symbolic number in Judeo-Christian culture.
> *Appearing often in the Bible and other sacred texts.*

Simply replacing the period with a comma will correct the problem:

> Seven is a symbolic number in Judeo-Christian culture, appearing often in the Bible and other sacred texts.

❷ Does the sentence have a subject?

In standard English, all sentences (except commands) must have a grammatical subject.

> *Linda* has two dogs. *One of them* is a black lab.

Sometimes a fragment can be corrected by simply inserting an appropriate subject and making other related changes:

> Most of today's sitcoms are not about families in suburbia.
> *Rather, they are*
> ~~But rather~~ *about young adults in the big city.*

Sometimes simply changing the punctuation and making the fragment part of the previous sentence will correct the error:

> *but*
> Most of today's sitcoms are not about families in suburbia ~~But~~ *rather about young adults in the big city*.

By removing the period after *suburbia*, you enable *most of today's sitcoms* to serve as the subject for the rest of the sentence, thereby eliminating the fragment.

❸ Are the dependent phrases or clauses connected to a main clause?

Check to be sure that word clusters beginning with a subordinating conjunction (such as *because, although,* or *if*) or a relative pronoun (such as *which, who,* or *that*) are connected or subordinated to a main subject and predicate.

12b Connect dependent clauses

Dependent clauses have a subject and a predicate but are linked to a main clause with a subordinating conjunction (such as *because, although,* or *if*) or a relative pronoun (such as *which, who,* or *that*). Because dependent clauses depend on their connection to a main clause for their meaning, they cannot stand alone. Therefore, if you begin a clause with a subordinating conjunction or relative pronoun and then end it with a period or semicolon before connecting it to a main clause, you have produced a fragment, not a sentence. In the following sentence, changing the semicolon to a comma allows the *Before* clause to serve as a dependent clause linked to *I must first discuss . . .* , the main clause.

> *Before I delve into critically analyzing the characters*; I must first discuss the opening sequence.

Relative clauses also need to be connected to a main clause. In the following sentence, the solution is simply to eliminate the period, joining the two clauses:

> *may*
> What seems annoying to me. ~~May~~ not bother you at all.

12c   Connect phrases

Phrases are similar to clauses except that they lack full verbs. Phrases can be used as modifiers, subjects, objects, or complements—but never as sentences. Make sure that all of your phrases are connected to main clauses.

Many nations began to process their own food, minerals, and other
raw materials, ~~Using~~ *, using* foreign aid and investments to back their efforts.

COMMA SPLICES AND RUN-ON SENTENCES

Joining two independent clauses with a comma creates a **comma splice**. Putting two independent clauses together without a conjunction or any punctuation creates a **run-on sentence** (or fused sentence).

Run-on sentences are incorrect in standard English and are often confusing to readers. There are four main ways to correct comma splices and run-on sentences:

- Turn one clause into a subordinate clause.
- Add a comma and a coordinating conjunction.
- Separate the clauses with a semicolon.
- Separate the clauses with a period.

> http://ccc.commnet.edu/grammar/runons.htm
> All you need to know about comma splices and run-on sentences, with exercises

 WebLink

12d   Turn one clause into a dependent clause

Often the best way to correct a comma splice or run-on sentence is to convert one of the two clauses into a dependent clause. This can be done by using either a subordinating conjunction (such as *while, although, because,* or *if*) or a relative pronoun (such as *which, that,* or *who*).

> The best keyboard for one-handed users is the Dvorak keyboard, *which* has a more convenient layout than the standard QWERTY keyboard.

Sometimes this technique may require switching the two clauses around:

> *Because* it has a more convenient layout than the standard QWERTY keyboard, the best keyboard for one-handed users is the Dvorak keyboard.

12e Separate clauses with a comma and a coordinating conjunction

If the two parts of a comma splice or run-on sentence are of equal importance, you can put a comma and a coordinating conjunction (such as *and, or, but, nor,* or *yet*) between them:

> *, but*
> An eagle once flew past our house ˄ I only got a brief glimpse of it.

Simply inserting a comma in a run-on sentence is not enough, for that only produces another error (a comma splice); you must also insert a conjunction.

12f Separate independent clauses with a semicolon

If the two parts of a comma splice or run-on sentence are of equal importance, you can insert a semicolon between them.

> *;*
> Desktop computers usually have bigger screens than laptops do/ laptops are easier to carry around.

If you use a conjunctive adverb such as *however, therefore,* or *for example,* be sure to place the semicolon before it:

> *;*
> Laptops are coming down in price/ *therefore,* more people are buying them.

12g   Separate independent clauses with a period

Often the easiest way to correct a comma splice or run-on sentence is by inserting a period between the two independent clauses:

> Dvorak keyboards put the most frequently typed characters within easy
>   *. They*
> reach~~, they~~ are often used in speed-typing competitions.

13   Subject-Verb Agreement

Subjects and verbs should agree in number; that is, they must both be either singular or plural. "He go to work at nine o'clock" is ungrammatical because *he* is singular and *go* (in the third person) is plural. Here are some rules on subject-verb **agreement**.

13a   Use plural verbs with plural subjects, singular verbs with singular subjects

He goes to work at nine o'clock.
We see each other later in the day.

With a modified subject, be sure the verb agrees with the simple subject.

> Meg's circle of friends gives her a lot of support. [*Circle* is the simple subject
> of the phrase *Meg's circle of friends.*]

13b Use plural verbs with most compound subjects

Compound subjects refer to two or more people, places, or things and are formed with the conjunction *and*. In most cases, compound subjects have a plural sense and thus require plural verbs.

WebLink
http://ccc.commnet.edu/
grammar/sv.agr.htm
A great guide to subject-verb
agreement, complete with
quizzes and exercises

Geography and history are my favorite subjects.

13c Make the verb agree with the closest part of a disjunctive subject

A **disjunctive subject** consists of two nouns or pronouns joined by *or* or *nor*. The verb in a sentence with such a subject agrees with the second part of the subject.

Either my sister or my parents are coming.

Neither my parents nor my sister is coming.

If the singular verb sounds awkward to you with such a mixed subject, you can switch the two parts of the subject and use the plural form of the verb:

Neither my sister nor my parents are coming.

13d After subjects like *each* and *none*, use a singular verb

Indefinite pronouns include *anybody, everyone, nothing, each,* and *much*. Unlike regular pronouns, they do not necessarily refer to any particular person or thing. Most indefinite pronouns are grammatically singular. Therefore, when used as subjects, they should have singular verbs.

No one is here.

Something needs to be done about this.

Each of the candidates is giving a short speech.

A few indefinite pronouns, including *both* and *others*, are plural and therefore require plural verbs. Other indefinite pronouns, such as *some, all, any, more,* and *none*, can be used with either singular or plural verb forms, depending on what they refer to.

All of the members were at the meeting. [*All* refers to plural *members.*]

All of their attention was directed at her. [*All* refers to singular *attention.*]

13e Use a singular verb with collective nouns like *team* and *committee*

Collective nouns are words such as *team, faculty, jury,* and *committee,* which can have either a singular or a plural sense depending on whether they refer to the group or to the individuals within the group (see 10a-1). These nouns usually take singular verbs.

The team is doing better than expected.

The band seems to be road-weary.

To emphasize the plural sense of collective nouns, simply insert an appropriate plural noun.

The band members seem to be road-weary.

13f Use a singular verb with nouns like *athletics* and *economics*

Words such as *mathematics, athletics, politics, economics, physics,* and *news* look like plural nouns because of the *s* ending. However, these nouns are usually singular in meaning and thus require singular verbs.

Economics is my favorite subject.

The news from Lake Wobegon always interests me.

13g Be sure a linking verb agrees with its subject

Sometimes you may find yourself faced with a sentence of the form "X is Y," in which the subject X is singular and the subject complement Y is plural, or vice versa. In such cases, the linking verb should agree in number with the subject, not with the subject complement (see 10b-3).

> Her main <u>interest</u> <u>is</u> boys.
>
> <u>Boys</u> <u>are</u> her main interest.

In a sentence beginning with *here* or *there* and some form of the verb *be*, the true (grammatical) subject is usually the noun that immediately follows the *be* verb form.

> There <u>are</u> some <u>people</u> at the door.
>
> Here <u>is</u> the <u>address</u> you were looking for.

14 ▶ Misplaced and Dangling Modifiers

Modifiers are words, phrases, or clauses that qualify other words, phrases, or clauses. Used properly, modifiers can make writing richer and more precise.

14a   Position modifiers close to the words they modify

For maximum clarity, modifiers should be placed as close as possible to (ideally, right next to) the words they modify.

Unlike George,
  ₐKramer does not need the approval of anyone. ~~unlike George~~.

frequently

Businesses ˄publish the URLs for their Web sites ~~frequently~~ in advertisements.

14b   Avoid ambiguity

A modifier that is not carefully positioned may mislead the reader into the wrong interpretation.

Idaho Teen Sentenced to Life for Murder of Parents Showing No Remorse

http://www.uottawa.ca/academic/ arts/writcent/hypergrammar/ msplmod.html

How not to use misplaced and dangling modifiers in your writing

It sounds like he killed them because they showed no remorse! The following version, with the modifier (*showing no remorse*) placed next to the word it modifies (*teen*), makes the intended meaning clearer:

Idaho Teen, Showing No Remorse, Sentenced to Life for Murder of Parents

14c   Try to put lengthy modifiers at the beginning or end

When a lengthy modifier is placed in the middle of a sentence, it tends to disrupt the basic structure (subject-verb-complement) of the sentence. By moving such modifiers to the beginning or end of the sentence, you preserve the basic structure and make the sentence more readable.

MODIFIER IN THE MIDDLE OF THE SENTENCE

A television network usually, *after it airs a documentary*, makes the film available to groups for a nominal rental fee.

REVISED

After it airs a documentary, a television network usually makes the film available to groups for a nominal rental fee.

14d   Avoid disruptive modifiers

English sentences are made up of subgroupings of words, such as the verb and its object or the word *to* and the rest of the infinitive construction. When modifiers are inserted into these subgroupings, there is a risk of interrupting and obscuring the vital connections between key words.

❶ Modifiers between the verb and its object

Readers like to be able to move easily through the main predicate of a sentence, going from verb to object without interruption. For this reason, it is best to avoid inserting any interupting modifiers between the verb and its object.

> *quickly*
> The magician ₍ₐ₎ shuffled ~~quickly~~ the cards.

❷ Split infinitives

Some readers prefer to see both parts of an infinitive construction (*to escape*) together, as in "He hoped *to escape* easily." Other readers will accept a one-word interruption between parts, or split infinitive, as in "He hoped *to* easily *escape*." Almost all readers have some difficulty comprehending an infinitive construction when its parts are split with a longer phrase, as in "He hoped *to* very easily and quickly *escape*."

SPLIT INFINITIVES REVISED

> *go*
> Star Trekkers hope to ₍ₐ₎ *boldly, loyally, and optimistically* ~~go~~ where none have gone before. [With all due respect for the original motto, too many modifiers splitting the infinitive here interrupt the sense of the sentence.]

14e   Avoid dangling modifiers

A mistake that plagues many writers is the use of the **dangling modifier**, an introductory verbal phrase that does not have a clear referent.

> Running down the hall, an elderly patient collided with Nurse Summers.

Was it the elderly patient who was running down the hall? That's how it appears from this sentence. If it was Nurse Summers who was running down the hall, the sentence should be rewritten with the modifying phrase next to *Nurse Summers*.

> Running down the hall, Nurse Summers collided with an elderly patient.

15 ▶ Faulty Shifts

Readers expect writers to use a consistent focus, time frame, and tone. Writers should try to satisfy this expectation by avoiding unnecessary shifts.

15a Avoid shifts in focus

The *focus* of a piece of writing is what or whom the writing is about. It is indicated usually by the choice of point of view, as expressed by a singular or plural subject pronoun: first person (*I, we*), second person (*you*), or third person (*he, she, it, they*). A first-person focus is an appropriate point of view for personal narratives and informal correspondence; a second-person focus is appropriate for instructions; a third-person focus is appropriate for most academic, professional, and other types of formal writing. Shifting from one focus to another can be confusing to readers.

> You should start writing a paper well before the deadline; otherwise, ~~one~~ *you* may end up doing it at the last minute, with no chance to revise it.

15b   Avoid unnecessary shifts in verb tense and mood

Verb tense indicates the time frame of an action (see 11j). Unless you are

WebLink

http://owl.english.purdue.edu/
handouts/esl/esltensyerb.html
How to avoid inappropriate
shifts, of verb tense.

describing a situation where there is a natural or logical difference in time frames, it is best to use the same verb tense throughout.

> In 1995, the median pay for full-time female workers in the United States was $22,497, while the median pay for males was $31,496.
>
>   *made*
> In other words, women ~~make~~ 71 cents to a man's dollar.

There are three **moods** in English: indicative, imperative, and subjunctive. The **indicative mood** is used for facts and assertions, the **imperative mood** for commands, and the **subjunctive mood** for conditions that are contrary to fact (see 11o). If you mix moods in the same sentence, you may confuse your readers.

INCONSISTENT MOOD

> If China were a democracy, it will have elections at periodic intervals.

REVISED

> If China *is* a democracy, *it will have* elections at periodic intervals.
> [Both verbs are in the indicative, suggesting a factual assertion.]

> If China *were* a democracy, it *would have* elections at periodic intervals.
> [Both verbs are in the subjunctive, indicating a contrary-to-fact condition.]

15c   Avoid shifts in tone

Tone refers to the writer's attitude toward the subject matter or the audience. It can be formal or informal, ironic or direct, friendly or hostile, and so on.

Since readers need to get a clear sense of what the writer's attitude is, a writer should strive to maintain a consistent authorial tone.

INCONSISTENT TONE

> The world of folklore and fairy tales is one that attracts adults and children alike. As adults, we look back fondly on childhood cartoons and still get a kick out of 'em.

REVISED FROM COLLOQUIAL TO FORMAL

> The world of folklore and fairy tales is one that attracts adults and children alike. As adults, we look back fondly on childhood cartoons and find them as enjoyable as ever.

15d   Avoid mixed constructions

Mixed constructions result when a writer starts a sentence in a certain way but then changes track and finishes it differently. The two parts of the sentence end up being incompatible—and confusing to the reader.

MIXED   In the world created by movies and television makes fiction seem like reality.

REVISED   The world created by movies and television makes fiction seem like reality.

OR   In the world created by movies and television, fiction seems like reality.

15e   Create consistency between subjects and predicates

Subjects and predicates should always harmonize, both logically and grammatically. When they do not, the result is faulty predication.

FAULTY   Writer's block is when you cannot get started writing.

In this sentence, a noun (*writer's block*) is compared to an adverb of time (*when . . .*).

N   N

REVISED   *Writer's block is a condition* in which you cannot get started writing.

15f Avoid unmarked shifts between direct and indirect discourse

Direct discourse is language that is taken word for word from another source and thus is enclosed in quotation marks. **Indirect discourse** is language that is paraphrased and therefore is *not* enclosed in quotation marks. If you shift from one mode to the other, you may have to alter not only punctuation but also pronouns and verb tenses so as not to confuse your readers.

CONFUSING   Agassiz, the legendary Swiss scientist and teacher, once said I cannot afford to waste my time making money. [Without quotation marks, this statement seems to refer to two different people: Agassiz and the writer.]

REVISED   Agassiz, the legendary Swiss scientist and teacher, once said that *he could not* afford to waste his time making money. [By signaling indirect discourse, the change of pronouns and verb tense makes it clear that Agassiz is referring only to himself.]

part 5

Effective Sentences and Words

16 Clarity of Sentence Structure

Readers today often are under time pressure and are not willing to spend valuable minutes trying to decode a piece of writing. Writers should accommodate their readers by making their writing as clear and concise as possible.

CLARITY AND CONCISENESS

There are several techniques that you can use for writing as clearly as possible, including these:

- Avoiding excessively long sentences
- Avoiding unnecessary repetition and redundancy
- Eliminating wordy phrases
- Avoiding a noun-heavy style
- Choosing precise words
- Making comparisons complete and clear

16a Avoid excessively long sentences

Sentences that are more than about twenty-five words long can sometimes be difficult for a reader, especially if the sentences are complicated.

Despite their significance in contemporary society, social movements seldom solve social problems, because in order to mobilize resources a movement must appeal to a broad constituency, which means that the group must focus on large-scale issues that are deeply embedded in society.

This sentence is forty-two words long. These three shorter sentences say the same thing and are much easier for the reader to understand:

Despite their significance in contemporary society, social movements seldom solve social problems. To mobilize resources, a movement must appeal to a broad constituency. This means that the group must focus on large-scale issues that are deeply embedded in society.

16b   Avoid unnecessary repetition and redundancy

A certain amount of repetition is necessary, both for emphasis and to maintain focus. Repetition is especially useful for linking one sentence to another. However, unnecessary repetition will only clutter your writing and irritate readers.

Life offers many lessons, ~~about life~~.

Redundancy is the use of words that could be left out without changing the meaning of the sentence. Saying that something is *blue in color* is redundant, because readers already know that blue is a color.

16c   Eliminate wordy phrases

Many commonly used phrases are unnecessarily long. If you can replace them with no loss of meaning, you should do so.

~~In a very real sense,~~ ^Ttrickle-down economics ~~exhibits a tendency~~ *tends* to trickle up, benefiting only the rich.

Wordy phrases	*Concise phrases*
as a matter of fact	in fact
at the present time	today

at this point in time   now
due to the fact that   because

16d   Avoid a noun-heavy style

A noun-heavy style is characterized by many more nouns than verbs. It tends to make excessive use of the verb *be* (*am, are, is, was, were*) and have strings of prepositional phrases.

NOUN-HEAVY   Thomas Jefferson was not a believer in the divinity of Jesus Christ and was the author of a version of the Four Gospels that involved the removal of all references to "miraculous" events.

MORE VERBAL   Thomas Jefferson did not believe in the divinity of Jesus Christ and wrote a version of the Four Gospels from which he removed all references to "miraculous" events.

16e   Choose words that express your meaning precisely

Good writing conveys its meaning efficiently, with precision. Such precision is achieved largely through the careful selection of words. Minimize your use of vague nouns like *area, aspect, factor, kind, nature, situation, sort, thing,* and *type,* as well as your use of vague adjectives like *bad, good, interesting, nice,* and *weird* and vague adverbs like *basically, completely, definitely, really,* and *very.*

http://www.wisc.edu/writing/
Handbook/ClearConcise
Senternces.html.
A resource for writing clear and
concise sentences

WebLink

     Democracy   *an*
~~A democratic type of government basically~~ requires ~~a pretty~~ informed citizenry.

16f   Make comparisons complete and clear

Comparative constructions inherently involve two terms: "*A* is _____er than *B*.*" In formal writing, you should make both terms of the comparison explicit.

INCOMPLETE   Talk radio has become a popular form of entertainment because it gets people more involved. [More involved than what?]

COMPLETE   Talk radio has become a popular form of entertainment because it gets people more involved than most other media do.

COORDINATION AND SUBORDINATION

In any piece of writing, readers will instinctively look for the most important points. By emphasizing these points and deemphasizing others, writers make their main points easier to locate in the text and thereby make their writing more readable.

Two important ways to create emphasis are through coordination and subordination of sentence elements. Remember, *form should reflect content*. If two related ideas are equally important, *coordinate* them by putting them on the same grammatical level. If they are not equally important, put the less important idea in a grammatically *subordinate* form.

16g   Look for a way to combine closely related sentences

Writing that contains one short sentence after another not only is unpleasantly choppy but also fails to emphasize some sentences more than others.

TOO CHOPPY

I was born and raised in a small midwestern town. It was easy to make friends. I got to know a lot of people. I was able to achieve almost all of my goals. I could do almost anything I wanted to.

This paragraph is so choppy that it is hard to get a sense of the writer's main point. You can solve this problem by noticing that several pairs of sentences are closely related and combining these sentences.

REVISED VERSION

I was born and raised in a small midwestern town. It was easy to make friends, *and so* I got to know a lot of people. *Since* I could do almost anything I wanted to, I was able to achieve almost all of my goals.

16h Coordinate related sentences of equal value

Coordination is the pairing of sentences or sentence elements by putting them in the same grammatical form and linking them via a coordinating conjunction, conjunctive adverb, or semicolon. The coordinating conjunctions are *and, but, or, nor, for, so,* and *yet.*

USE OF A COORDINATING CONJUNCTION

A high-fiber diet appears to lower the risk of certain cancers, *so* the National Cancer Institute recommends consuming 25 to 35 grams of fiber a day.

Conjunctive adverbs provide another way of giving equal emphasis to two conjoined sentences. The conjunctive adverbs include *however, consequently, therefore, thus, hence, furthermore, moreover, afterward, indeed*, and *otherwise.* They often are preceded by a semicolon.

USE OF A CONJUNCTIVE ADVERB

The 1928 Pact of Paris offended nobody, since it included no compulsory machinery of enforcement; *hence* the European nations rushed to sign it.

A coordinate relationship also can be created between two sentences simply by using a semicolon.

USE OF A SEMICOLON

People are affected by social forces sometimes far removed from their immediate perceptions; they perceive only a relatively small portion of the influences that play on them.

16i   Subordinate less important ideas

To combine two closely related but unequal ideas, use **subordination**: put the more important idea in a main clause and the lesser one in a subordinate clause. Subordinate clauses are typically set off by subordinating conjunctions (such as *although, because, if, since, though, unless, until*, and *while*) or by relative pronouns (such as *that, which, who, whom*, and *whose*).

USE OF A SUBORDINATING CONJUNCTION

Even though we know that advertisers are "out to get us," we do not make much of an attempt to refute their messages.

Using hands-on experience is one of the best ways of learning, *as* it helps the student learn on a more interactive level.

USE OF A RELATIVE PRONOUN

The Great Lakes cool the hot winds of summer and warm the cold winds of winter, *which* gives the state of Michigan a milder climate than some of the other north central states.

PARALLELISM

Whenever a writer links two or more words or phrases that have similar roles in a sentence, readers expect to see them in the same grammatical form. When the linked similar words or phrases are balanced and in the same form, the result is called **parallelism** (or *parallel structure* or *parallel form*). When Benjamin Franklin wrote "A penny saved is a penny earned," he was using parallelism. The adjective *saved* parallels in content and form the adjective *earned*.

Not only can parallelism make writing more elegant, but it can also direct the reader's attention to important structural relationships among ideas within sentences. Putting two elements in parallel form makes it easy for the reader to compare them.

16j   Put parallel content in parallel form

Words and phrases that are linked by the coordinating conjunctions *and, but, or,* or *nor* are often parallel in content. In such cases, they should also be parallel in form, using the same grammatical structure.

> *cease* and *desist*   [Both verbs]
>
> *hook, line,* and *sinker*   [All nouns]
>
> *of the people, by the people,* [and] *for the people*   [All prepositional phrases]

16k   Make all items in a list or series parallel

Whenever you present any kind of listing in formal or academic writing, whether it is a formatted list such as an outline or just a series of items in a sentence, all of the items should be in the same grammatical form.

NONPARALLEL SERIES REVISED

> The last decades of the nineteenth century through the early decades of the twentieth marked a period when Americans confronted rapid industrialization, a communications revolution,
>
> *the growth of big business*
> and ~~big business was growing.~~   [A third noun phrase is put into the series to replace the distracting nonparallel clause.]

16l   Use parallelism with *both/and*, *either/or*, etc.

Whenever you use correlative conjunctions such as *both/and, either/or, neither/nor,* or *not only/but also,* you are lining up two sentence elements for comparison. Those elements therefore require parallel grammatical form.

> Either *we go full speed ahead* or *we stop right here.*

16m   Use parallelism for comparisons or contrasts

A comparison or contrast involves two statements or terms that are seen as somehow equivalent; indeed, it is this equivalence that allows them to be compared. These two statements or terms should therefore be parallel. A good example of contrasting parallelism occurs in Shakespeare's *Julius Caesar*, where Brutus tries to justify, before the citizens of Rome, his assassination of Caesar:

> Not that I loved Caesar less, but that I loved Rome more. Had you rather Caesar were living, and die all slaves, than that Caesar were dead, to live all free men?
>
> —*Julius Caesar*, 3.2.21–24

VARIETY

Good writers always try to make their writing interesting, not only in content but also in style. This is where variety comes in. By varying your style, you change the rhythm of your writing and keep your readers interested. If you write the same kind of sentence over and over again, you are likely to put your readers to sleep.

16n   Vary sentence length

One of the easiest and most effective ways to alter the rhythm of your writing is to vary the length of your sentences. You do not have to change length with every sentence, but you certainly should do so from time to time. Note how Barbara Kingsolver does it in the opening paragraph of *The Bean Trees*:

> I have been afraid of putting air in a tire ever since I saw a tractor tire blow up and throw Newt Hardbine's father over the top of the Standard Oil sign. I'm not lying. He got stuck up there. About nineteen people congregated during the time it took for Norman Strick to walk up to the Courthouse and blow the whistle for the volunteer fire department.
>
> —Barbara Kingsolver, *The Bean Trees*

16o Vary sentence structure

Another way to alter the rhythm and cadence of your writing is by varying the structure of your sentences. Based on clause structure, sentences can be divided into four basic types:

A **simple sentence** contains one independent clause and no other clauses.

A **compound sentence** contains two independent clauses.

A **complex sentence** contains one independent clause and one or more subordinate clauses.

A **compound-complex sentence** contains two independent clauses and at least one subordinate clause.

16p Avoid excessive repetition

Repetition always draws attention. If you use it deliberately to create parallelism or emphasis, that is fine. But if you use it for no particular reason, you will only draw attention to your repetitiveness—not a good way to liven up your style!

17 Word-Processing Tools and Online Resources

Among the conveniences of using a computer for writing is the ready access to editing and formatting tools, which are found in any standard word-processing program. But these tools must be used with care. This chapter discusses such word-processing tools as style and grammar checkers and style templates. (Thesauruses and dictionaries are discussed in Chapter 24.) The chapter concludes with a brief discussion of the kinds of Internet sites that can be helpful in sentence revision.

17a Use a style or grammar checker with caution

A typical style or grammar checker will scan your document and apply whatever rules it has been programmed to observe. Since the rules reflected in the programs are taken from traditional grammar and style books, computerized style and grammar checkers are similar in the kinds of things they flag, such as long sentences, archaic words, sexist expressions, double negatives, sentence fragments, and passive verbs.

❶ Problems overlooked by style and grammar checkers

Style and grammar checkers can be useful in pointing out potential trouble spots, but they have serious shortcomings. First, they overlook many potential problems. Of all the stylistic and grammatical problems illustrated in the examples in Part 4 of this book, for example, our style and grammar checker could identify only a third. It was unable to identify any of the pronoun reference problems in Chapter 11, any of the modifier problems in Chapter 14, or any of the consistency problems in Chapter 15.

❷ Nonconstructive suggestions made by style and grammar checkers

Style and grammar checkers flag many things that are not problematic. In some cases, the computer misreads the sentence. In other cases, it applies a rule too simplistically. For example, if your style or grammar checker flags a passive-voice verb, you may decide that you should change it to active voice. But using the passive voice is not always wrong; indeed, sometimes it is the better choice. Many stylistic choices depend on things that a computer cannot assess.

17b Use style templates

Style templates are preset formats for common types of documents, such as business letters, memos, résumés, and reports. Whenever you need to write these types of documents, you can get off to a quick start by just opening the template (usually in the FILE menu).

Style templates are handy tools, especially if you frequently write the same kind of document. But do not hesitate to modify any template that is preset in your computer.

17c Use other applications for sentence revision

In addition to style and grammar checkers and style templates, word processors offer a number of special functions that can be used in revising sentences or paragraphs. For example, a revisions program allows you to insert changes in a draft and then compare what the draft looks like with and without the changes.

One of the most useful word-processing features is the SEARCH, or FIND, feature (often located in the EDIT menu). This feature allows you to specify the context in which you want to find a specific word or letter combination.

17d Consult Internet resources for writing help

Chapters 1, 2, and 4 describe how to use the Internet and networking resources for research and for peer exchanges or collaborative work associated with the composition process. In addition, the Internet can provide you with help in writing and revising sentences and in developing stronger word usage. Some of this help can come from useful and entertaining Web sites that offer advice on all kinds of grammar, usage, and vocabulary topics (many of these are identified in the WebLink boxes throughout this book).

18   Choosing the Right Words and Avoiding Biased Language

Since meaning is conveyed through words, a writer's choice of words, or **diction**, is crucial. Choose your words carefully, and you will make your writing clearer and more interesting; choose your words carelessly, and you may leave your readers frustrated.

Writers sometimes use the power of language negatively to express bias, the one-sided (usually negative) characterization of an entire group. Writers should try at all times to avoid bias in their writing.

18a   Choose words that have the right meaning

The **denotation** of a word is its basic dictionary meaning. The verbs *walk, stroll, hobble, saunter, promenade, hike, march*, and *tramp* all have the same basic meaning, or denotation—"to move by alternately putting one foot in front of the other, always having at least one foot on the ground." Unlike these words, the verbs *run, walk*, and *crawl* differ in denotation. Your first obligation in choosing words is to select ones that accurately denote whatever idea you are trying to convey. For example, if Julie *crawled* to the nearest house, it would be a misrepresentation to say that she either *walked* or *ran*.

❶ General statements versus specific details

All good writing involves a mixture of general statements and specific details. General statements establish main points, while specific details make these points precise, vivid, and memorable. Good writers thus continually make choices among words whose denotations range from general to specific. For example, instead of deciding whether Julie *ran, walked*, or *crawled*, the writer could have chosen to use a verb with a more general meaning, such as *go*.

❷ Abstract versus concrete nouns

Abstract nouns have broad, often vague denotations, like *power, romance,* and *democracy.* Such words refer to concepts rather than to tangible objects. **Concrete nouns** refer to things that are available to the senses—things that we can see, touch, hear, smell, or taste. For example, *raccoon, Statue of Liberty,* and *radishes* all bring to mind tangible, concrete objects. As with general statements and specific details, you should aim for a mixture of the abstract and the concrete.

18b　Choose words that have the right connotation

Connotations are the extra nuances of meaning that distinguish otherwise synonymous words. *Walk, stroll, hobble, saunter, promenade, hike, march,* and *tramp* all are considered synonyms, yet each brings to mind a somewhat different image. Make sure that you are aware of a word's connotations before you use the word; otherwise, the message you convey to your readers may be very different from the one you intended.

> http://www.uottawa.ca/academic/
> arts/writcent/hypergrammar/
> diction.html
> A hyperlinked discussion of
> denotation, connotation, catch
> phrases, and clichés

18c　Find the right level of formality

Words vary in their level of formality, or register, from very formal to colloquial. Always listen to what you are writing, to make sure that you consistently use words in the appropriate register.

❶ Formal, academic vocabulary

Virtually all writing you do for school and college assignments (except for special cases such as creative writing or personal narratives) should be in a fairly formal register, as is this handbook. Formal, academic vocabulary consists largely of words derived from Latin and Greek—words like *inevitable*, *hypothesis*, *perception*, *theory*, and *superfluous*—which is why you are tested on such words when you take the SAT or ACT exam.

2 Informal vocabulary

Informal words are those you might use in ordinary, everyday contexts such as talking with friends and sending email messages.

Although informal vocabulary is sometimes acceptable in formal writing, you should generally try to use the more formal equivalents where possible.

Informal	*Formal*	*Informal*	*Formal*
friendly	amicable	do again	repeat
worn out	exhausted	go faster	accelerate

18d   Avoid jargon, slang, or dialect

There are many versions of English, only one of which—Standard Edited English—is represented in this book. Standard Edited English is the version most widely used in academic and professional contexts and most widely understood around the world. Other versions, including jargon, slang, and dialect, are valuable in their own right. However, they are less widely understood, and thus you should refrain from using them except with audiences composed of fellow "insiders."

Jargon is any technical language used by professionals, sports enthusiasts, hobbyists, or other special-interest groups. By naming objects and concepts that are unique to a group's special interests, jargon facilitates communication among members of the group.

Used by teenagers and other subcultures, slang is a deliberately colorful form of speech whose appeal depends on novelty and freshness. For this reason, slang terms tend to be short-lived, quickly giving way to newer, fresher replacements.

A dialect is the type of speech used by a specific social, ethnic, or regional group. Dialects typically have a distinctive accent, many unique words and expressions, and even some grammatical patterns that differ from those of Standard Edited English.

18e   Avoid pretentiousness

College students are continually exposed to the discourse of academics—professors, scholars, textbook writers—who have spent most of their adult lives developing a large vocabulary and an embellished style of writing. If you find yourself tempted to imitate this style of discourse, do so with great caution. You are at risk of sounding pretentious.

18f   Use figurative language

Figurative language uses words in nonliteral, creative ways to enhance the reader's understanding. Two of the most common figures of speech are **simile** and **metaphor**, both of which attempt to explain the unfamiliar by comparing it to the familiar.

When they are still fresh, metaphors add sparkle to writing. But over time, if they are used heavily, they become worn out and lose their charm. An overused metaphor is called a *cliché*. Some examples of clichés are *white as a sheet, barking up the wrong tree*, and *climbing the ladder of success*. Good writers avoid clichés in formal writing.

18g   Avoid biased gender references

In the past, men and women had distinctly different roles in society. Language developed accordingly. A doctor was presumed to be male; in the relatively few cases where a doctor happened to be a woman, she was referred to as a *woman doctor*. A nurse, on the other hand, was presumed to be female; gender was indicated only in those relatively few cases involving a *male nurse*.

Stereotyping can arise unwittingly through the careless use of examples

http://owl.english.purdue.edu/handouts/general/gl_nonsex.html
Guidelines for nonsexist language from the Purdue Online Writing Lab

WebLink

and illustrations. Try to vary the roles of men and women in your examples, thereby broadening the spectrum of possibilities for both sexes.

❶ Gender-specific nouns

In general, do not use gender-marked terms in situations where a person's gender should not be of any relevance.

Sexist	*Gender-neutral*
businessmen	businesspersons
foreman	supervisor
manpower	personnel, staff

❷ Generic pronouns

Traditionally, *he, him,* and *his* were used as **generic pronouns** to refer to all members of a group, regardless of sex. A sentence such as "Everyone should pay attention to his spelling" would supposedly apply to both males and females. But using only masculine words as generic pronouns has been found to be discriminatory in its psychological effects.

18h Avoid biased language about race and ethnicity

Language that either intentionally or unintentionally discriminates against people because of their race or ethnicity is a form of verbal aggression. Unbiased writers reject the sort of disparaging stereotyping evident in ethnic jokes and in sweeping statements about ethnic groups.

18i Avoid biased language about age and other differences

In our youth-oriented culture, it is not uncommon to hear demeaning references to age. Indeed, the adjective *old* often is used gratuitously as a way of denigrating others. Avoid age-related stereotypes and expressions in examples and jokes.

Occupational, religious, political, regional, socioeconomic, and disability-related groups are among the many other groupings in our society that are subject to stereotyping. As with ethnic groups, it is generally best to refer to such groups in ways that they themselves prefer. For example, most people with physical disabilities prefer to be called *physically disabled* rather than *handicapped,* and most people who clean buildings prefer the title of *custodian* rather than that of *janitor.* Such preferences should be respected.

part

6 Punctuation

19 End Punctuation

There are three ways to punctuate the end of a sentence: with a period, a question mark, or an exclamation point.

THE PERIOD

WebLink → http://www.uottawa.ca/academic/arts/writcent/hypergrammar/endpunct.html. All about end punctuation.

The period is used to indicate the end of a statement, to punctuate initials and abbreviations, and to mark basic divisions in units and computer names.

19a Use a period to mark the end of a statement

Sometimes called a "full stop," the period is most commonly used to mark the end of a sentence. Just make sure before you place the period that the words form a *complete grammatical sentence*, or else you will be creating a sentence fragment (see Chapter 12).

19b Use periods to punctuate initials, abbreviations, unit divisions, and computer names

Initials that stand for middle names or first names take periods:

Mary W. Shelley   O. J. Simpson   F. Scott Fitzgerald

Leave one space after each period when punctuating initials in names. Most abbreviations ending in lowercase letters take periods.

Ms.   St.   Jan.
Dr.   apt.   Inc.

Basic divisions in money, measurements, email addresses, and file names all take periods:

$99.50   3.2 meters   13.5 gallons
English.paper.doc   michael.okiwara@u.cc.utah.edu

19c Avoid common misuses of periods

1. *Do not use a period to mark just any pause.* If you insert a period whenever you want readers to pause, you run the risk of creating sentence fragments (see 12a–b). Consider this example:

   http://stipo.larc.nasa.gov/sp7084/sp7084ch3.html
   A description of all uses of the period and the question mark

   Attempts to challenge reactionary political views are often branded as "politically correct" by those same reactionaries. *Who support only their own versions of "free speech."* [The second sentence is a fragment.]

2. *Do not use periods with acronyms and other all uppercase abbreviations.*

   CA   NBA   USA   UN   FBI
   NOW   NAACP   MS-DOS   CD-ROM   JFK

3. *Do not use periods at the end of stand-alone titles or headings.* The title of this chapter and its numbered headings are examples of stand-alone titles and headings, respectively.

4. *Do not use periods at the end of sentences within sentences.*

The famous proverb, "A penny saved is a penny earned," was coined by Benjamin Franklin.

5. *Do not use periods after items in a formatted list (unless all are complete sentences).* The table of contents for this handbook is an example of a formatted list. Only when all the items in the list are sentences is it acceptable to have periods after the individual items.

THE QUESTION MARK

Question marks are placed after direct questions, whereas periods follow indirect questions. Do not use a comma or a period after a question mark.

19d   Use a question mark after a direct request

REQUESTING
INFORMATION   Who wrote *Jesus Christ, Superstar* ?

ASKING FOR
CONFIRMATION   It's a complicated situation, isn't it ?

MAKING A
POLITE REQUEST   Could you please be a little quieter ?

❶ Using question marks with direct and indirect quotations

If the direct quotation is a question and it is at the end of the sentence, put the question mark inside the quotation marks.

The police officer asked me, "Do you live here ?"

Do not use a question mark after an indirect question. An indirect question is the writer's rewording of a question posed by someone else.

A tourist asked me where the Lincoln Memorial was.

❷ Using question marks in a series

It is acceptable to put a question mark after each independent item in a series, even if it is not a full sentence.

> Will our homeless population continue to grow? Stay about the same? Get smaller?

If the question is an either/or type, put a question mark only at the end of the sentence.

> Are you coming with us or staying here?

THE EXCLAMATION POINT

Exclamation points are used to show strong emotion, including amazement and sarcasm. Do not use a comma or a period after an exclamation point.

19e   Use an exclamation point to signal a strong statement

The statement marked with an exclamation point does not have to be a full sentence.

AN OUTCRY OR COMMAND	Oh! Watch out!
STRONG EMPHASIS	People before profits!
ASTONISHMENT	Imagine reading this news report and not getting upset!
SARCASM	And the cigarette companies claim that smoking is not addictive!

20 The Comma, Semicolon, and Colon

Three of the most common and most useful punctuation marks in the English language—and also the most difficult to master—are the comma, semicolon, and colon. This chapter provides some guidelines (not rules) for the use of these punctuation marks.

THE COMMA

One way to show a close relationship between independent clauses is with a comma.

20a Use a comma to set off an introductory phrase or clause

http://owl.english.purdue.edu/
handouts/grammar/
g_comma.html
A discussion of the main uses
of the comma, accompanied
by good proof reading
strategies and exercises

When readers start to read a sentence, one of the first things they do (unconsciously) is try to locate the grammatical subject. Help them do this by setting off with a comma any potentially distracting words that *precede* the subject.

Using a comma after an introductory element is especially important in cases where it is needed to prevent possible confusion.

CONFUSING   Soon after starting the car began making funny noises.
CLEAR   Soon after starting, the car began making funny noises.

Use a comma before *and, but, or,* etc., to separate independent clauses

The combination of a comma and a coordinating conjunction (*and, but, or, nor, for, so, yet*) is one of the most common ways of connecting independent clauses.

> Members of a mainstream culture often feel threatened by a counterculture, *and* they sometimes move against it in an attempt to affirm their own values.

When you are using a coordinating conjunction to link phrases rather than clauses, you generally do not insert a comma.

> Acupuncture has proved effective for treating chronic pain /and for briefly blocking acute pain.   [The simple parallel phrases need no separation; a revision removes the unnecessary comma.]

However, writers sometimes insert a comma to create more separation between the two parts.

> Acupressure is similar to acupuncture, but does not use needles.   [The contrastive phrase is separated with a comma.]

20c   Use commas between items in a series

A series of three or more items should have commas after all but the last item.

> My patriotic neighbor says that *red, white, and blue* are his favorite colors.

Occasionally in journalistic writing or in company names composed of three or more personal names, the last comma in the series—called the **serial comma**—is omitted.

> My uncle used to work for *Pierce, Fenner and Smith.*

Use commas to separate coordinate adjectives

When the adjectives in a series could be arranged in any order or could be (but are not) strung together with the use of *and*, they are termed **coordinate**

adjectives. To show their loose relationship and also to avoid confusion with adjectives that cumulate in a particular order to modify each other, separate coordinate adjectives with commas.

A *rusty, dented, broken-down* car was left behind.

In this example, each adjective modifies the word *car*.

20e Use commas to set off nonessential phrases or clauses

A nonessential element, or **nonrestrictive element**, provides an extra piece of information that can be left out without changing the basic meaning of the sentence. Always use punctuation to set off nonessential, or nonrestrictive, elements from the rest of the sentence. (By contrast, elements that are essential, or restrictive, are always integrated into the sentence without separating punctuation.) Nonessential elements are most commonly set off with commas; however, parentheses or dashes may also be used.

Lung cancer, *the leading cause of cancer deaths in the United States,* kills more than 153,000 Americans each year.   [A nonessential appositive is set off with commas.]

Unless the nonessential element begins or ends the sentence, be sure to use *two* commas to set it off, not just one.

20f Use commas to set off words like *however, therefore,* and *furthermore*

Conjunctive adverbs include the words and phrases *however, therefore, consequently, thus, furthermore, on the other hand, in general,* and *in other words*. They serve as useful transitional devices, helping the reader follow the flow of the writer's thinking. By enclosing conjunctive adverbs in commas, you give them more prominence, clearly marking a shift in thinking.

Resistance-training exercises cause microscopic damage to muscle fibers, which take twenty-four to forty-eight hours to heal; *therefore,* resistance-training programs require at least one day of rest between workouts.

20g   Use commas with dates, place names and addresses, titles and degrees, and numbers

When writing a date in the traditional American format of month, day, and year, set off the year by placing a comma after the day.

> John F. Kennedy died on November 22, 1963, in Dallas, Texas.

Do not use a comma if only the month and year are given.

> John F. Kennedy died in November 1963 in Dallas, Texas.

Do not use a comma when writing a date in the European format of day, month and year.

> John F. Kennedy died on 22 November 1963 in Dallas, Texas.

Use commas after all major elements in a place name or address. However, do not put a comma before a ZIP code.

> Aretha Franklin was born in Memphis, Tennessee, on March 25, 1942.
>
> Alfredo's new address is 112 Ivy Lane, Englewood, NJ 07631.

Use commas to set off a title or degree following a person's name.

> Stella Martinez, MD, was the attending physician.

Use a comma in numbers of five digits or more, to form three-digit groups. In a number of four digits, the comma is optional.

> 2,400 OR 2400
>
> 56,397
>
> 1,000,000

Exceptions: Do not use commas in house numbers, ZIP codes, telephone numbers, account numbers, model numbers, or dates.

20h   Use commas with speaker tags

If you are quoting someone and using a speaker tag (such as *he said, according to Freud*, or *notes Laurel Stuart*), put a comma between the tag and the quotation.

Thomas Edison said, "Genius is 1 percent inspiration and 99 percent perspiration."

 Use commas with markers of direct address

Put commas around words that indicate that you are talking directly to the reader: words such as *yes* or *no*, the reader's name (*Bob*), question tags (*don't you agree?*), or mild initiators (*Well, Oh*).

Yes, the stock market is likely to turn around.

Do you really think, *Grace,* that Professor Wilson will postpone the test?

 Avoid misuse of commas

1. *Never use a single comma between the subject and predicate.* When a complex subject begins a sentence, writers sometimes feel inclined to add an inappropriate comma that splits the subject and predicate.

FAULTY COMMA REVISED

Numerous psychological and social factors / have a strong influence on how people age.

2. *Never put commas around restrictive elements.* **Restrictive elements** are phrases or clauses that are essential to defining the meaning of the sentence. They should not be set off with commas.

Consumers / who are considering using a hospital or clinic / should scrutinize the facility's accreditation.   [In this sentence, the writer is referring not to all consumers but only to those who are considering using a hospital or clinic.]

3. *Avoid using commas with cumulative adjectives.* Adjectives that accumulate before a noun, each one modifying those that follow, are called **cumulative adjectives**. Their modifying relationships, which depend on their order, are likely to be confused by the separating commas that are common with adjectives in a coordinate series.

CONFUSING COMMAS REVISED

The suspect was seen driving a *small/new/Italian/luxury/*car.

4. *Avoid putting a comma before* than. Resist the urge to heighten a comparison or contrast by using commas to separate the *than* clause from the rest of the sentence.

FAULTY COMMA REVISED

Beating our archrival was more important/than getting to the state playoffs.

5. *Avoid using a comma after a subordinating conjunction.* A comma should not be used to separate a subordinating conjunction from its own clause; it should be used before the conjunction to separate the entire clause from the rest of the sentence.

FAULTY COMMA REVISED

Although/the car is fifteen years old, it seems to be in good shape.

6. *Never use a comma before parentheses or after a question mark or exclamation point.* A comma is superfluous with an opening parenthesis, question mark, or exclamation point.

UNNECESSARY COMMA REVISED

Muhammad was born in Mecca/(now in Saudi Arabia) and founded the religion of Islam around AD 610.

7. *Do not insert a comma before a list.* Resist the urge to punctuate before a listed series.

UNNECESSARY COMMA REVISED

Some countries, such as/the Netherlands, Sweden, and Denmark, have very compassionate welfare systems.

8. *Do not use a comma in a two-item series.* Although commas are needed to separate three or more items in series, separating two items with a comma is unnecessary and distracting.

UNNECESSARY COMMA REVISED

Her outfit used strong contrasts between red / and blue.

THE SEMICOLON

A semicolon is used mainly when two clauses have a coordinate relationship—that is, when they convey equally important ideas (see 16h) but do not have a coordinating conjunction (*and, but, or, not, for, so, yet*) between them.

 20k Use a semicolon to separate independent clauses

 http://web.wisc.edu/writing/ Handbook/Semicolons.html A complete guide to semicolons

When there is no coordinating conjunction, related independent clauses should be connected with a semicolon rather than a comma.

The first panacea for a mismanaged nation is inflation of the currency; the second is war. Both bring a temporary prosperity; both bring a permanent ruin.

—Ernest Herningway, *Notes on the Next War*

 20l Use a semicolon to separate independent clauses linked by a conjunctive adverb

If you separate two independent clauses with a conjunctive adverb such as *however, therefore,* or *nevertheless,* you must use a semicolon.

More than 190 countries belong to the United Nations; *however,* only 5 of them have veto power.

 20m Use semicolons in a series with internal punctuation

A **complex series** is one that has internal punctuation. Normally, commas are used to separate items in a series; however, if the individual items contain commas, it can be difficult for readers to determine which commas are internal to the items and which commas separate the items. In these cases, semicolons are used to separate the items.

> I have lived in Boulder, Colorado; Corpus Christi, Texas; and Vero Beach, Florida.

 20n Place semicolons outside quotation marks

Semicolons are always positioned outside quotation marks.

> Those who feel abortion is not a woman's prerogative say they are "pro-life"; those who feel it is say they are "pro-choice."

 20o Avoid common semicolon errors

1. *Do not use a semicolon between an independent clause and a dependent clause or phrase.* Dependent clauses or phrases are linked to independent clauses most often by commas, not semicolons.

> When we say that a country is "developing"; we imply that it
> is backward in some way.   [The introductory clause should be linked by a comma, not a semicolon.]

2. *Do not use a semicolon to introduce a list.* Use a colon instead (but see 20p).

> Utah has five national parks; Arches, Bryce, Canyonlands, Capitol Reef, and Zion.

THE COLON

In formal writing, the colon is used mainly after a general statement to announce details related in some way to the statement. These details may be a list of items, a quotation, an appositive, or an explanatory statement.

20p Use a colon to introduce a list

In using a colon to introduce a list or an appositive, be sure that the introductory part of the sentence is a grammatically complete clause.

WebLink
http://www.uottawa.ca/
academic/arts/writcent/
hypergrammar/colon.html
An introduction to using the-
colon

In creating a macro, you can assign it to any one of three places: the toolbar, the keyboard, or a menu.

20q Use a colon to set off a second independent clause that explains the first

Rock climbing is like vertical chess: in making each move up the wall, you should have a broad strategy in mind.

Note: You may begin the clause after the colon with either an uppercase letter or a lowercase letter.

Although both the colon and the semicolon can be used to separate independent clauses, they cannot be used interchangeably. A semicolon is used when the two clauses are balanced; a colon is used when the second clause is a specification of the first.

COLON   Blessed are the pure in heart: for they shall see God.

SEMICOLON   My soul shall make its boast in the Lord; the humble shall hear of it and be glad.

20r Use a colon to introduce a quotation

When a colon is used to introduce a quotation, the part of the sentence that precedes the colon should be grammatically independent.

In *Against Empire*, Michael Parenti states his concern about American foreign policy: "We should pay less attention to what U.S. policymakers profess as their motives—for anyone can avouch dedication to noble causes—and give more attention to what they actually do."

20s Use colons in titles

Colons are often used in the titles of academic papers and reports. The part of the title that follows the colon is called the subtitle. It usually provides a more explicit description of the topic than the title does.

> *Nature and the Poetic Imagination: Death and Rebirth in "Ode to the West Wind"*

 20t Use colons in business letters and memos

In business letters and memos, colons are used in salutations (*Dear Ms. Townsend:*), to separate the writer's initials from the typist's initials (*TH:ab*), and in memo headings (*To:, From:, Date:, Subject:, Dist:*).

20u Use colons in numbers and addresses

Colons are used in biblical citations to distinguish chapter from verse (*Matthew 4:11, Genesis 3:9*), in clock times to separate hours from minutes and minutes from seconds (*5:44 p.m.*), in ratios (*3:1*), and in Web site addresses (*http://www.fray.com*).

 # 21 The Apostrophe and Quotation Marks

THE APOSTROPHE

The apostrophe is used to indicate possession, to alert the reader to contractions and omitted letters, and to form certain plurals.

21a   Use apostrophes with nouns to indicate possession

In its grammatical sense, **possession** refers to ownership, source, or some other special relationship between two nouns. With singular nouns, possession is usually indicated by attaching *'s* to the end of the noun.

Sue Ellen's jacket   yesterday's bad weather

There are two exceptions to this rule:

1. If the rule would lead to awkward pronunciation, the extra *s* may be omitted: *Euripides' plays, Moses' laws, Mister Rogers' Neighborhood*.

WebLink

http://www.grammarbook.com/ punctuation/apostro.html
An excellent guide to apostrophes, including exercises

2. In names of places, companies, and institutions, the apostrophe is often omitted: *Robbers Roost, Kings County, Starbucks, Peoples Republic*.

For plural nouns ending in *s*, form the possessive by just adding an apostrophe at the end:

the Browns' car   the Yankees' star pitcher   my parents' friends

For plural nouns not ending in *s*, form the possessive by adding *'s*:

women's rights   children's section   sheep's wool

❶ Avoiding apostrophes with possessive personal pronouns

Personal pronouns never take apostrophes to indicate possession. They have their own possessive forms: *its, his, her/hers, your/yours, their/theirs, our/ours, my/mine.*

Be careful not to confuse *its* and *it's*. The former is possessive; the latter is a contraction for *it is.*

❷ Showing possession with multiple nouns

With multiple nouns, use apostrophes according to your intended meaning. If you want to indicate joint possession, add an apostrophe only to the last of the nouns:

Obama and Biden's campaign

If you want to show *separate* possession, put an apostrophe after each of the nouns:

Omar's, Gretchen's, and Mike's birthdays

21b Use apostrophes to indicate contractions and omitted letters

In casual speech, syllables are sometimes omitted from common word combinations. For example, *cannot* becomes *can't*. In formal writing, such **contractions** are generally inappropriate. In much informal writing, however, such as email messages and personal letters, contractions are quite common. Just be sure to punctuate them correctly with an apostrophe.

| will not → won't | should not → shouldn't | it is → it's |
| I am → I'm | you have → you've | they are → they're |

21c Use apostrophes to mark certain plural forms

When a letter or symbol is used as a noun, the usual way of pluralizing nouns (adding an *s* or *es*) does not work well: "There are four *ss* in *sassafras*." In such cases, an apostrophe can help out.

There are four *s*'s in *sassafras*.

Both the Modern Language Association and the American Psychological Association recommend omitting the apostrophe in forming plurals like the following:

the 1990s   several IOUs   a shipment of PCs

QUOTATION MARKS

The primary use of quotation marks is to acknowledge other people's words and statements. Using quotation marks is especially important in academic writing, which puts special value on the ownership of ideas.

21d Use quotation marks for exact direct quotations

Quotation marks should be placed around any words, phrases, or sentences that you have borrowed from someone else (unless the quotations are so lengthy that you prefer to set them off as an indented block).

> In *The End of Work*, Jeremy Rifkin said, "In the years ahead, more than 90 million jobs in a labor force of 124 million are potentially vulnerable to replacement by machines."

❶ Paraphrasing or quoting indirectly

A summarization, restatement, or paraphrase of a statement made by someone else is a form of **indirect discourse**, and quotation marks are not used. Putting quotation marks around words that were not those of the speaker or writer would be extremely misleading.

MISLEADING QUOTATION MARKS REVISED

> Rifkin argues that in the future more than two-thirds of the American workforce could be displaced by automation.

❷ Setting off long quotations in block form

A long quotation (more than about four lines) should be set off as an indented block without quotation marks.

> Rifkin sees this reduction of the workforce as having profound social effects:

> The wholesale substitution of machines for workers is going to force every nation to rethink the role of human beings in the social process. Redefining opportunities and responsibilities for millions of people in a society absent of mass formal employment is likely to be the single most pressing social issue of the coming century.

21e Use quotation marks to suggest skepticism about a term

Sometimes you may find yourself writing about a concept that you think does not deserve the respect other people are giving it. In such cases, you can convey your skepticism by putting the name of the concept in quotation marks.

> Although many people consider the family the foundation of American society and talk about a return to "family values" as a desirable objective, it is clear that the modern American family looks quite different from families of previous generations.

21f Use quotation marks to indicate shifts of register

Quotation marks can be used occasionally to set off a colloquial term from the more formal discourse surrounding it.

> One should always try to avoid an inflexible, "cookie-cutter" approach to rhetorical criticism.

21g Use quotation marks when citing titles of short works

When referring by title to short stories, book chapters, poems, essays, songs, and other brief works, enclose the titles in quotation marks.

> "Smells like Teen Spirit" is a '90s classic.

21h Follow standard practice in using other punctuation with quotations

1. *Put commas and periods inside the end quotation mark.* Standard American editorial practice calls for commas and periods to be placed as shown in the following passage:

> "The definition of community implicit in the market model," argues Patricia Hill Collins, "sees community as arbitrary and fragile, structured fundamentally by competition and domination."

http://ccc.commnet.edu/
grammar/marks/quotation.htm
A description of all uses of
quotation marks, with links to
exercises and related topics

2. *Put colons and semicolons out-side the end quotation mark.*

One critic called 1990 "the year in which rock & roll was reborn": the fusing of metal and rap by groups like Living Colour and Faith No More broke down racial barriers in a way reminiscent of early rock & roll.

3. *Put other punctuation marks inside the end quotation mark if they are part of the quotation; otherwise, put them outside the end quotation mark.* Question marks, exclamation points, dashes, parentheses, and other punctuation marks should be positioned according to meaning.

PART OF QUOTED TITLE

Whitney Houston's "How Will I Know?" entered the pop charts at number one.

PART OF SENTENCE

What do you think of controversial songs like "Deep Cover" and "Cop Killer"?

4. *Use single quotation marks (' ') for quotation marks within quotation marks.*

Garofalo notes that "on cuts like 'JC' and 'Swimsuit Issue,' Sonic Youth combined an overt sexuality with uncompromisingly feminist lyrics about women's issues."

5. *Introduce quotations with the punctuation standard grammar calls for.* The sentence or phrase you use to introduce a quotation should be punctuated according to the grammatical relationship between the introduction and the quotation. If the introduction is not a grammatically complete sentence, do not use any punctuation.

The conservative Parents Music Resource Center maintained that heavy metal was "the most disturbing element in contemporary music."

22   Other Punctuation Marks

Parentheses, dashes, brackets, ellipses, and slashes can all be used, in moderation and in proper contexts, to clarify meaning and add interest to writing.

http://stipo.larc.nasa.gov/sp7084/sp7084ch3.html
A full discussion of parentheses, dashes, brackets, ellipses, and slashes

WebLink

PARENTHESES

Parentheses are indispensable to formal writing. Be sure, though, not to overuse them.

22a   Use parentheses to insert nonessential comments

Usually, parenthetical comments—clarifications, asides, examples, or other extra pieces of information—are embedded within sentences. They can be as short as a single word or as long as an entire sentence.

> For most right-handed people, the left hemisphere of the brain controls manual skills and language (and vice versa for most left-handed people).

Another common use of parentheses is in documentation. The scientific reference style calls for inserting reference citations in parentheses within sentences (see Chapters 6 and 7). This parenthetical style is the preferred method of the MLA, APA, and CSE.

22b Do not overuse parentheses

Parentheses are so handy that you may be tempted to overuse them. Resist the temptation. Too many parentheses can make it difficult for readers to follow the main train of thought.

22c Use parentheses around letters or numbers to set off embedded lists

Listed phrases or clauses embedded in a longer sentence may be itemized with numbers or letters placed within parentheses.

> Socialism has three essential components: (1) the public ownership of the means of production, (2) central planning, and (3) distribution of goods without a profit motive.

DASHES

Dashes are an informal kind of punctuation, with several uses and some misuses. You can create a dash either by typing two hyphens, which some word processors will then convert into a solid dash, or by opening the special character or symbol feature of your word-processing program and selecting the full-length dash (called the "em dash").

22d Use dashes to highlight extra informational comments

Dashes set off internal, informational comments in a more emphatic way than parentheses do.

> Public decision makers have a tendency to focus mostly on the more obvious and immediate environmental problems—usually described as "pollution"—rather than on the deterioration of natural ecosystems upon whose continued functioning global civilization depends.

22e   Use dashes to set off important or surprising points

If not overused, dashes can be a dramatic way to set off an inserted comment.

> While the Marshall Islanders continue to wrestle with the consequences of nuclear testing, a new proposal is on the table that will make the islands a dumping ground for American garbage—literally.

 22f   Confine yourself to one pair of dashes per sentence

Dashes, like parentheses, can be overused. If you need to add more than one informational comment to a sentence, use commas or parentheses around the other comments. Too many dashes in a paragraph are a sign of poorly integrated ideas.

BRACKETS

Brackets are an important editorial device for providing proper context for the quoted or cited material used in research writing.

22g   Use brackets to insert editorial comments or clarifications into quotations

Quotations represent someone's exact words. If you choose to alter those words (because of a misspelling in the original quotation or to add explanatory information, for example), you

must indicate that you have done so by putting brackets around the alterations.

> "One of the things that will produce a stalemate in Rio [*the site of the 1992 UN conference on the environment*] is the failure of the chief negotiators, from

both the North and the South, to recognize the contradictions between the free market and environmental protection."

The Latin word *sic* (meaning "so" or "thus") indicates a mechanical error—for example, an error of grammar, usage, or spelling—in a quotation. Enclose it in brackets.

"Any government that wants to more and more restrict freedoms will do it by financial means, by creating financial vacums [*sic*]."

 ### 22h Use brackets to acknowledge editorial emphasis within a quotation

When you quote a passage, you may want to emphasize a certain part of it that is not emphasized in the original. You can do so by underlining or italicizing that part and then, at the end of the passage, acknowledging the change by writing *emphasis added* or *italics mine* between brackets.

 ### 22i Use brackets for parenthetical comments within other parenthetical comments

If one parenthetical comment is nested within another, punctuate the inner one with brackets to distinguish it from the outer one.

The spectacular palace that King Louis XIV built at Versailles (located 19 kilometers [12 miles] west of Paris) required 35,000 workers and twenty-seven years to construct.

ELLIPSES

An ellipsis (plural: ellipses) is a series of three periods, used to indicate a deletion from a quotation or a pause in a sentence. An ellipsis consists of three *spaced* periods (. . .), not three bunched ones (. . .). If you end a quoted sentence with an ellipsis, use a fourth period to indicate the end of the sentence.

"The notion of literature as a secular scripture extends roughly from Matthew Arnold to Northrop Frye . . . ."

The *MLA Handbook for Writers of Research Papers*, 6th edition, notes that some instructors advocate placing brackets around any ellipses you insert in a quoted passage. However, it prefers using brackets only to distinguish your own omissions from those of the quoted author.

 Use an ellipsis to indicate a deletion from a quotation

The sentence with an ellipsis should not be significantly different in meaning from the original sentence, nor should it be ungrammatical.

> "Practically any region on earth will harbor some insect
>
> species—native or exotic—that are functioning near the limits
>
> of their temperature or moisture tolerance."

An ellipsis can be used to mark a deletion from either the middle or the end of a sentence but not the beginning of a sentence.

 Use an ellipsis to indicate a pause in a sentence

To mark a pause for dramatic emphasis in your own writing, use an ellipsis.

> I was ready to trash the whole thing . . . but then I thought better of it.

SLASHES

Slashes serve a variety of purposes in both formal and informal writing.

 Use slashes to separate lines of poetry quoted within a sentence

If you are quoting lines of poetry without setting them off in separate lines as they appear in the poem, put a slash (with a space on each side) between the lines.

> Gerard Manley Hopkins's poetry features what he called "sprung rhythms," as can be heard in these lines from "The Windhover": "No

wonder of it: sheer plod makes plow down sillion **/** Shine, and blue-bleak embers, ah my dear, **/** Fall, gall themselves, and gash gold-vermilion."

 Use a slash to show alternatives and to indicate a fraction

Slashes are used in expressions like *either/or*, *pass/fail*, *on/off*, *win/win*, and *writer/editor*. (In some cases, a hyphen may be used instead.) Readers may object, though, if you overuse them. The expressions *he/she*, *his/her*, and *s/he* are admirable attempts at gender neutrality, but many people dislike their phonetic clumsiness. We suggest you use *he or she* and *his or her* or find other ways of avoiding sexist pronouns.

Fractions that would be set in formal mathematics on separate lines also can be shown on one line, with a slash dividing the numerator from the denominator:

1/3   3/8   2-2/5

part 7

Mechanics and Spelling

23

Capital Letters, Italics, Abbreviations, and Numbers

CAPITAL LETTERS

Capital (uppercase) letters are used to indicate the start of a new sentence. They also are used for proper names, proper adjectives, and some abbreviations.

> **23a** Capitalize the first word of all free-standing sentences

Sentences like the one you are now reading should always start with a capital letter. Sentences that are embedded in other sentences, however, may or may not start with a capital letter, depending on the situation.

http://stipo.larc.nasa.gov/sp7084/
sp7084ch4.html
A discussion of almost all uses of
capital letters

WebLink

If a sentence occurs in parentheses within another sentence, the first word of the parenthetical sentence should not be capitalized:

> Major league baseball no longer seems to enjoy the civic loyalty it used to
>
> *for*
> (~~For~~ example, several teams have threatened to leave their cities if new facilities are not built).

If a sentence occurs as a quotation within another sentence and is set off by a colon, comma, or dash, the first word should be capitalized:

> *Vegetarians*
> Rush Limbaugh once said, "~~vegetarians~~ are a bunch of weaklings who wouldn't be able to bench-press 50 pounds after one of their meals."

However, if the quotation is not set off by a colon, comma, or dash, the first word should be lowercase:

> *vegetarians*
> Rush Limbaugh once said that "~~v~~egetarians are a bunch of weaklings who wouldn't be able to bench-press 50 pounds after one of their meals."

Question fragments can also be capitalized.

> Will the stock market keep booming? Level off? Take a dive?

If you are quoting a poem, capitalize the first letter of each line (if the original did so).

> Long as the heart beats life within her breast
>   Thy child will bless thee, guardian mother mild,
> And far away thy memory will be blest
>   By children of the children of thy child.
>
> —Alfred, Lord Tennyson, 1864

23b   Capitalize all names, associated titles, and proper adjectives

Capitalize the first letter of any name, title, or proper adjective referring to a particular person, place, or thing.

1. *Capitalize names and associated titles of people.*

   Ruth Bader Ginsburg   Dr. Harris
   Professor Mixco   Dale Earnhardt, Jr.

2. *Capitalize place names.*

   San Diego, California   the Rockies
   Lake Michigan   Maple Street

Note: Compass points (north, southwest) are capitalized only when they are incorporated into a name (North Carolina) or when they function as nouns denoting a particular region (the Southwest).

3. *Capitalize the names of historical events.*

World War II	the Middle Ages
Reconstruction	the My Lai Massacre

4. *Capitalize the names of days, months, holidays, and eras.*

Monday	the Reagan Era
April	Thanksgiving

Note: Seasons of the year are not capitalized:

last fall   winter sports   spring semester

5. *Capitalize the names of organizations, companies, and institutions.*

Common Cause	Intel Corporation
the United Nations	Alameda Community College

6. *Capitalize the names of products and unique objects.* In most cases, only the first letter of each word in an object or product name is capitalized:

the Hope Diamond	the North Star
the *Titanic*	the Boeing 767

Some manufacturers, especially in the computer industry, use intercaps (internal caps):

WordPerfect	QuarkXPress
HotJava	GlobalFax

7. *Capitalize religious, national, and ethnic names.*

Catholicism	Chicano
the Koran	Passover

8. *Capitalize adjectives based on proper nouns.*

American football	Jewish literature
French history	Southern hospitality
Newtonian physics	Islamic tradition

23c Capitalize all significant words in titles

In titles of books, poems, articles, plays, films, and other cultural works, every word except articles (*a, an, the*), conjunctions, and short prepositions should be capitalized. The first word of the title and of the subtitle should be capitalized, even if it is an article, conjunction, or short preposition.

The Joy Luck Club	"Ode to the West Wind"
Death of a Salesman	"Learning in Context: A Qualitative Study"

23d Follow the owner's preferences in capitalizing email addresses and URLs

Although most of the Internet is not case-sensitive, there are two important reasons for writing email and Internet addresses exactly as the owners do. First, some parts of Net addresses, such as the URL pathnames that follow the first single slash, *are* case-sensitive. Second, some Netizens use uppercase and lowercase letters to make important distinctions in their addresses.

ITALICS

In published documents, *italic* typeface is used for a number of purposes. (*Note*: Although most word-processing programs permit the selection of an italic typeface, many instructors prefer that students use *underlining* instead of italics in their papers, as underlined letters and words stand out more than italicized ones.)

23e Italicize titles of independent creative works

Titles of books, magazines, digital magazines ("e-zines"), newspapers, and other creative products that are independently pack-aged and distributed to a public audience should be written with italics or un-derlining. Here are some examples:

http://ccc.commnet.edu/grammar/italics.htm
A brief guide to using italics and underlining

WebLink

BOOKS   *The Scarlet Letter* or The Scarlet Letter
MAGAZINES   *National Geographic* or National Geographic
E-ZINES   *Salon* or Salon

23f Italicize URLs and email addresses

When writing an Internet or email address in the body of a text, use underlin-ing or italics.

> Helpful information about current congressional legislation can be found at *http://thomas.loc.gov/*. The email address is *thomas@loc.gov*.

23g Italicize names of vehicles

Names of particular vehicles, not types of vehicles, should be underlined or italicized. These include the names of spacecraft, airplanes, ships, and trains.

> *Voyager 2* or Voyager 2
> *Spirit of St. Louis* or Spirit of St. Louis

23h   Italicize foreign words and phrases

In general, it is best to avoid using foreign words and phrases when writing in English. However, if you need to use a foreign expression (for example, because there is no good English equivalent), write it with underlining or italics and, if possible, provide a brief English explanation.

> My Dutch friends say they like being in a *gezellig* environment, one that has a lot of human warmth.

Foreign words that have become common English words should *not* be italicized or underlined. Here are some examples:

machete (Spanish)	judo (Japanese)
sauerkraut (German)	coffee (Arabic)

23i   Italicize words, letters, and numbers referred to as such

When you write a word, letter, or number so as to talk about it as a word, letter, or number, use underlining or italics.

> Many people misspell the word *misspell*; they write it with only one *s*.

Underlining or italics is also appropriate for a word you are about to define. (Alternatively, boldface type can be used.)

> Before starting up a cliff, rock climbers sometimes like to get *beta*—advice from someone who has already done the climb.

ABBREVIATIONS

Abbreviations include shortened versions of words (*Mr., Rev., fig.*), initialisms formed from the first letters of a series of words (*FBI, NBC, IBM*), and acronyms, or initialisms that are pronounced as words (*OPEC, NASA, RAM*). In formal writing, abbreviations should be used sparingly. If you are not sure that readers will know what a certain abbreviation stands for, spell out the word the first time it is used and put the abbreviation in parentheses right after it:

> The Internet uses a domain name system (DNS) for all its servers worldwide.

23j Abbreviate titles, ranks, and degrees only before or after full names

Title before full name	Degree or rank after full name
Dr. Teresa Rivera	Derek Rudick, CPA
Prof. Jamie Smith-Weber	Young-Sook Kim, PhD

When titles or ranks are followed by only a surname, they should be spelled out:

General Powell   Professor Davis

23k Use abbreviations after numerical dates and times

The following abbreviations are commonly used in writing dates and times:

124 BC ("before Christ") OR 124 BCE ("before the common era")

AD 567 (*anno Domini*, or "year of our Lord") OR 567 CE ("common era")

9:40 a.m. (*ante meridiem*) OR 0940 hrs (military or international twenty-four-hour time)

4:23 p.m. (*post meridiem*) OR 1623 hrs

23l Use Latin abbreviations sparingly

The following abbreviations, derived from Latin, are appropriate in academic writing. Be careful, however, not to overuse them.

Abbreviation	Latin term	English meaning
cf.	*confer*	compare
e.g.	*exempli gratia*	for example

et al.	*et alii*	and others
etc.	*et cetera*	and so forth
i.e.	*id est*	that is
N.B.	*nota bene*	note well

23m Use acronyms and initialisms only if their meaning is clear

http://ccc.commnet.edu/
grammar/abbreviations.htm
A superb guide to
abbreviations

An initialism is an abbreviation formed from the first letters of a name—for example, *FBI* (for *Federal Bureau of Investigation*). Usually the letters are all capitalized. An **acronym** is an initialism that is pronounced as a word—for example, *ASCII, PAC, AIDS*. Some abbreviations, such as *JPEG, MS-DOS*, and *DRAM*, are *semi-acronyms*: part of the term is pronounced as one or more letters, the rest as a word (for example, "jay-peg"). As long as your audience knows what they mean and as long as you do not overdo it, there is nothing wrong with using such abbreviations where appropriate.

23n Avoid most other abbreviations in formal writing

Place names, including the names of states, countries, provinces, continents, and other localities, should not be abbreviated except in addresses and occasionally when used as adjectives (for example, in *U.S. government*). Organization and company names should not be abbreviated unless they are extremely familiar (*UNESCO, IBM, UCLA*) or the full name has first been given. Fields of study should not be abbreviated. Write *political science* (not *poli sci*) and *psychology* (not *psych*).

NUMBERS

When you are writing text and need to cite a number, keep in mind the following guidelines.

23o Use figures with abbreviations and conventionally numerical references

Time

| 7:00 a.m. | 0700 hrs | seven o'clock in the morning |
| 2:45 p.m. | 1445 hrs | two forty-five in the afternoon |

Dates

65 BC (or BCE)   AD 126 (or 126 CE)   the 1890s   May 15, 1996
from 1996 to 1998   1996–1998   1996–98

Money

$23.4 billion $12,566 $7.99   45¢   forty-five cents   one dollar

Rates of speed

| 55 mph | 33.6 bps |
| 200 MHz | 3000 rpm |

> http://owl.english.purdue.edu/
> handouts/esl/eslnumber.html
> An excellent guide to the use of
> numbers
>
> ◄ **WebLink**

Decimals and percentages

.05   5 percent (or 5%)

Telephone numbers

(617) 555-1284 [US]   +1 (617) 555 1284
                           [International]

Addresses

233 East 19th Street   PO Box 45   Route 66
New York, NY 10011

Divisions of books and plays

volume 2, chapter 11, pages 346–55
King Lear, act II, scene i, lines 5–7 or *King Lear* II.i.5–7
The Alchemist, act 2, scene 1, lines 5–7 or *The Alchemist* 2.1.5–7

23p   Write out other numbers that can be expressed in one or two words

One to ninety-nine

fifteen   twenty-two   eighty-four

Fractions

two-thirds   one-fourth   five-sixteenths

Large round numbers

thirteen hundred   four thousand   thirty million

Decades and centuries

the eighties (or the '80s)
the twenty-first century (or the 21st century).

23q   Write out numbers that begin sentences

FAULTY   18% of Americans believe that career preparation should begin in elementary school.

REVISED   Eighteen percent of Americans believe that career preparation should begin in elementary school.

When a number is too large to write out (more than two words), keep the numerical form but rearrange the sentence so as to avoid beginning with a number.

FAULTY   240,183 people could be fed for one year with the food we Americans waste in one day.

REVISED   We Americans waste enough food in one day to feed 240,183 people for one year.

23r   When one number modifies another, write one as a figure and the other as a word

We bought fourteen $25 tickets.
There were 75 twelfth-graders at the dance.

23s   Write related numbers in the same way

When comparing two or more numbers in the same sentence or paragraph, make the comparison easy to see by putting the numbers in the same form, as either words or figures.

> *900*
> It takes ~~nine hundred~~ hours of training to become a licensed hair braider in New York City but only 117 hours to become an emergency medical technician.

24   The Hyphen, Spelling, and Using a Thesaurus and Dictionary

THE HYPHEN

The hyphen (-) is typed as a single keystroke, with no space before or after. It differs from a dash, which is typed as two consecutive hyphens (--) and then usually converted by the computer into what looks like a long hyphen (—). The hyphen has two main functions: punctuating certain compound words and names (*self-destruct, fifty-fifty, Coca-Cola*) and dividing a word at the end of a line.

24a   Consult your dictionary on hyphenating compounds

A **compound** is a word made up of two smaller words. Sometimes these smaller words are connected by a hyphen (*screen-test*), sometimes they are separated by a space (*screen pass*), and sometimes they are fused (*screensaver*). There are no firm rules for determining how to write a particular compound, so it is best to check your dictionary.

24b Hyphenate compounds acting as adjectives before nouns

When a compound is placed in front of a noun to act as a modifier, it is usually hyphenated.

> I teach *seventh-grade* algebra.

Notice that the same compound, when placed after a noun, is *not* hyphenated.

> I teach algebra to the *seventh grade*.

WebLink http://www.grammarbook.com/ punctuation-hyphens.html
All about hyphens

Complex compounds are compounds made up of three or more words, like *cut-and-paste*, *ultra-high-density*, and *up-to-date*. When you hyphenate a complex compound, be sure to hyphenate all its parts—put hyphens between all the terms.

> I do a lot of *cut-and-paste* revising.

24c Hyphenate spelled-out fractions and numbers from twenty-one through ninety-nine

one-half   three-eighths   forty-four

24d Hyphenate to avoid ambiguity and awkward spellings

Some words, especially those with the prefix *re-*, *pre-*, or *anti-*, require hyphens to prevent misreadings, mispronunciations, and awkward-looking spellings:

> Now that Professor Muller has complicated the problem, we will have
>
> *re-solve*
> to ~~resolve~~ it.   [Without the hyphen, re-solve, "to solve again," would be read as resolve, "to deal with successfully."]

24e Use hyphens for end-of-line word division

In general, it is best to avoid dividing a word at the end of a line. But there are situations where word division is desirable. For example, if you are trying to arrange text in columns (in a brochure or résumé, for instance), end-of-line hyphenation may provide valuable extra space.

1. *Divide words only between syllables.* End-of-line hyphenation should occur only at syllable breaks.

2. *Avoid a second hyphen in a hyphenated word.* Words with prefixes like *self-*, *ex-*, and *all-* and complex compounds should not be hyphenated anywhere else.

   Jimmy Carter has set a new standard for civic activism by ex-~~presi-~~
   presidents
   ~~dents~~.

3. *Leave at least two letters on a line.* Do not divide a word so that a single letter is left hanging either on the first line or on the second line.

   emo-
   Stress management requires an examination of one's e-
   tional
   ~~motional~~ responses to others.

4. *Avoid consecutive lines ending in hyphens.* Ending three or more lines in a row with hyphens draws attention and looks ungainly.

   Admitting to your feelings and allowing them to be expressed through either communication or action is a stress-
   management technique that can help you through many difficult situations.

SPELLING

Modern English is a product of many other languages, including German, French, Latin, Greek, and Spanish. One unfortunate result of this hybridization is an irregular system of spelling that causes problems for many users of the language. If you are one of those people, be assured that you are not alone. However, it is important that you work on your spelling and keep trying to improve it. Many readers have little tolerance for bad spelling.

24f Use a spell checker

A computerized spell checker makes it easy to review for spelling errors. If you are not already doing so, you should routinely run a final spell check on any important document you write. Some word-processing programs allow you to set the spell checker so that it will identify possible misspellings either while you are typing or after you have finished.

Spell checkers are far from perfect. Sometimes they flag words that are spelled correctly (especially names), and sometimes they fail to flag words that are spelled incorrectly.

Identifying misspellings that the spell checker missed is a more difficult problem. Spell checkers will accept any word that happens to match a word form in its dictionary, even if the word is misused. The most effective ways to avoid this problem are by (1) mastering troublesome homophones; (2) guarding against common spelling errors; and (3) learning some general spelling rules and patterns.

24g Master troublesome homophones

Homophones are words that sound alike but are spelled differently and have different meanings. They are one of the most common causes of misspelling in English and cannot be detected by a spell checker. For this reason, you should study them and learn their differences, especially those listed here:

its	possessive pronoun
it's	contraction of *it is*
loose	adjective: "free, not tightly secured"
lose	verb: "fail to keep"
their	possessive form of *they*
there	adverb: "in that place"

they're	contraction of *they are*	

to	preposition
too	adverb: "also" or "excessively"
two	adjective and noun: "2"

who's	contraction of *who is*
whose	possessive form of *who*

your	possessive form of *you*
you're	contraction of *you are*

24h Guard against common spelling errors

Although a spell checker can flag many spelling errors for you, it is still worth learning the correct spelling of the most commonly misspelled words. Some of these words follow.

Commonly Misspelled Words

accidentally	environment	necessary
accommodate	exaggerate	occurred
achieved	exceed	parallel
basically	February	receive
committee	government	separate
definitely	manageable	until
dependent		

24i Learn general spelling rules and patterns

Although English is not the simplest language in the world to learn when it comes to spelling, it does have a number of general rules and patterns that make things easier.

❶ Prefixes

Prefixes are small word parts, like *re-*, *anti-*, and *pre-*, placed at the beginnings of words. Prefixes do not change the spelling of the root word: *anti-* added to *freeze* becomes *antifreeze*. In some cases, though, a hyphen is required: *anti-* plus *intellectual* is spelled *anti-intellectual*.

> mis- + spell = misspell
> un- + necessary = unnecessary

❷ Suffixes

Suffixes are small word parts, like *-age, -ence, -ing,* and *-tion*, placed at the ends of words. By adding suffixes to a root word such as *sense*, you can create different meanings: *sensitive, sensual, sensory, senseless*. In doing so, however, you must observe the following spelling rules.

1. If the word ends in a silent *e* and the suffix starts with a vowel, drop the *e*.

> imagine + -ation = imagination

There are some exceptions. Some words need to retain the *e* in order to be distinguished from similar words (*dyeing/dying*), to prevent mispronunciation (*mileage, being*), or to keep a soft *c* or *g* sound (*noticeable, courageous*).

2. If the word ends in a silent *e* and the suffix starts with a consonant, do not drop the *e*.

> require + -ment = requirement
> spine + -less = spineless

Some exceptions are *argument, awful, ninth, truly,* and *wholly*.

3. When adding a suffix to a word that ends in *y*, change the *y* to *i* if the letter preceding the *y* is a consonant.

> study + -ous = studious
> comply + -ance = compliance

Exceptions are words with the suffix *-ing*, which keep the *y* in all cases: *studying, carrying, drying, paying*.

4. In creating adverbs from adjectives, add *-ly* to the adjective unless the adjective ends in *ic*, in which case use *-ally*.

> silent + -ly = silently
> vile + -ly = vilely

5. In choosing between *-able* and *-ible*, use *-able* if the root word can stand alone; otherwise, use *-ible*.

> understand + -able = understandable
> change + -able = changeable
> vis- + -ible = visible

6. Double the final consonant of the root word if (a) the root word ends with a single accented vowel and a single consonant and (b) the suffix begins with a vowel.

> drop + -ed = dropped
> slim + -er = slimmer

❸ Plurals

English has several ways of forming plurals from singular nouns. Following are some rules for forming plurals.

1. For most words, add *-s*.

> tool, tools   minute, minutes

2. For words ending with *s, sh, ch, x,* or *z,* add *-es.*

> bus, buses   sandwich, sandwiches
> quiz, quizzes   [Note the doubled final consonant.]

3. For words ending with a consonant followed by *y,* change the *y* to *i* and add *-es.*

> enemy, enemies   strawberry, strawberries

4. For some words ending with *f* or *fe,* change the *f* or *fe* to *v* and add *-es.*

> half, halves   thief, thieves

Some exceptions are *belief, beliefs; chief, chiefs; proof, proofs;* and *motif, motifs.*

5. For compound nouns written as single words, add the plural ending as you would to an ordinary noun.

> laptop, laptops   database, databases

6. For compound nouns written as two or more words or hyphenated, add the plural ending to the noun being modified.

video game, video games   [The noun being modified is *game*.]
word processor, word processors   [The noun being modified is *processor*.]

Irregular plurals must be learned individually. Sometimes, an internal vowel must be changed to make a noun plural:

woman, women   mouse, mice

With some nouns derived from Latin or Greek, a final *us, um*, or *on* must be changed to *i* or *a*:

syllabus, syllabi   medium, media   criterion, criteria

Some nouns have the same form for both singular and plural:

deer, deer   species, species

❹ The "*i* before *e*" rule

The rule you had to memorize in elementary school is worth keeping in mind: "*i* before *e* except after *c* or when sounded like '*ay*,' as in *neighbor* or *weigh*."

I BEFORE E

achieve   field

EXCEPT AFTER C

ceiling   receive

OR WHEN SOUNDED LIKE "AY"

eight   vein

Some exceptions are *ancient, caffeine, conscience, counterfeit, either, foreign, height, leisure, neither, science, seize*, and *weird*.

USING A THESAURUS AND DICTIONARY

A writer needs tools, and two of the best are a good thesaurus and a good dictionary.

24j Use a thesaurus to find the exact word

Part of being a good writer is choosing words that accurately express your thoughts. A thesaurus is a listing of synonyms and antonyms that allows you to zero in on the exact word you are looking for.

❶ Electronic thesaurus

Today, most word-processing programs have a built-in thesaurus, which you can use as you write. (It is usually on the same menu as the spell checker.) You can also find thesauruses on the Internet. Or you can buy a thesaurus on a CD-ROM, either by itself or as a supplement to a dictionary.

❷ Traditional thesaurus

You should also feel comfortable using a thesaurus in traditional book form. The pocket-size versions are handy for carrying around; larger, desk-size thesauruses are found in all libraries and many offices. In many pocket-size thesauruses, the words are arranged alphabetically, as in a dictionary.

24k Use a dictionary to learn about words

Traditional printed dictionaries come in two types: pocket size and desk size. The pocket size is handy, but the desk size contains more complete information. Electronic dictionaries usually have as much information as desk-size types and can be found in CD-ROM format or on the Internet.

❶ Spelling, word division, and pronunciation

A typical dictionary entry begins with the main word, correctly spelled and divided into syllables: *ha-rass*. Knowing where to divide a word is helpful for typing if you do not use automatic hyphenation on your computer. If a word has two correct spellings, they are both listed, with the preferred spelling first. The word's pronunciation is indicated next, in parentheses: (hăr´əs, hə-răs´), with the preferred form first. Most modern dictionaries have a pronunciation key at the bottom of the page to help you decipher the pronunciation. For words of more than one syllable, a heavy accent mark (´) indicates which syllable

http://writing.colostate.edu/links/
index.cfm?category=writers
Direct access to the best online
dictionaries and thesauruses

should receive primary stress; some words have a secondary accent (´) as well. Some electronic dictionaries allow you to click on a button and get a voice recording of the correct pronunciation of the word.

❷ Parts of speech, word endings, and word senses

Next come symbols describing some aspect of the word—for example, what part of speech it is (such as a noun, verb, or adjective) or whether it is singular or plural. The most common abbreviations are these:

adj.	adjective	*intr.*	intransitive	*pron.*	pronoun
adv.	adverb	*n.*	noun	*sing.*	singular
aux.	auxiliary	*pl.*	plural	*suff.*	suffix
conj.	conjunction	*pref.*	prefix	*tr.*	transitive
interj.	interjection	*prep.*	preposition	*v.*	verb

Often an entry will include variants of the main word, showing different word endings.

Many words have more than one meaning, or sense. Each sense has a separate listing, generally preceded by a boldface number. In some dictionaries, these senses are arranged historically, according to when they entered the language; in other dictionaries, senses are listed according to current popularity, with the most commonly used sense appearing first.

❸ Etymology, related words, synonyms, and usage

Information about a word's origin, or etymology, is given in square brackets. This information can help you learn the word and use it accurately.

part 8 ESL Issues

25 Tips on Nouns, Articles, Verbs, Word Order, and Vocabulary

NOUNS AND ARTICLES

Articles (*a, an, the*) are important in the English language because they clarify what nouns refer to. There is a significant difference in meaning between "I found *a* new Web site" and "I found *the* new Web site." The first sentence introduces new information, while the second sentence implies that the new Web site is something the reader or listener already knew about. Articles can be used to mark other subtleties as well. Because many other languages do not use articles in this way, though, many nonnative speakers of English have trouble with articles.

25a Use the plural only with count nouns

To use articles correctly, you first need a clear understanding of the difference between count nouns and noncount nouns. Count nouns refer to things that have a distinct physical or mental form and thus can be counted, like *book, apple, diskette, scientist*, and *idea*. Count nouns can be enumerated and pluralized—for example, *eight books, three apples, several diskettes, two scientists*, and *many ideas*.

Noncount (or mass) nouns are words like *air, rice, electricity, excitement*, and *coverage* that do not have a distinct form as a whole. (Though each grain of rice may have a distinct form, rice as a mass quantity is variable in form.) Noncount

WebLink
http://leo.stcloudstate.edu/
grammar/countnon.html
Help with count and
noncount nouns

nouns are neither enumerated nor pluralized. No one would say *eight airs, three rices, several electricities, two excitements,* or *many coverages.* Noncount nouns are quantified with expressions like *a lot of, much, some,* and *a cup of*—for example, *some air, a cup of rice, much excitement,* and *a lot of coverage.*

25b　Use *the* for specific references

In deciding whether to use *the, a, an,* or no article at all, keep in mind the concept of specificity. Does the noun refer to some particular thing or set of things, or does it refer to something general? As mentioned in the introduction to this chapter, *"the* Web site" refers to a specific, unique Web site, whereas *"a* Web site" refers to any Web site.

❶ Using *the* with superlative adjectives

Adjectives like *best, worst,* and *most interesting* single out one particular thing among many.

❷ Using *the* with unique things

The past, the present, the sun, and *the solar system* all have unique identities. There is only one past, only one present, only one sun (in our solar system anyway).

> Thirty minutes after boarding, the plane was still on *the ground*.

❸ Using *the* with nouns followed by a modifier

Many nouns are followed by a phrase or clause that restricts the noun's identity.

> *The theory of relativity* was developed by Einstein.
> *The girl in the corner* is in my physics class.

❹ Using *the* to refer to something previously mentioned

Once something has been mentioned, it becomes part of the reader's knowledge. When you refer to it again, use *the* so that the reader knows that you are talking about the same thing.

I went shopping today and bought some beans, rice, and *chicken*. We can cook *the chicken* for dinner.

Note: For clarity or emphasis, the demonstrative adjective *this, that, those*, or *these* may sometimes be used instead of *the*.

❺ Using *the* to draw on shared knowledge

If you and your reader can draw on shared experience to identify something in particular, use *the* to mark it.

Please shut down *the computer* when you are done with it.

❻ Using *the* for contextual specificity

Sometimes the context of a situation allows you and your reader to identify something as unique. Consider, for example, the word *printer*. There are many printers in the world, but if you are writing about a computer and you want to mention the printer attached to it, use *the* to indicate that it is the only printer in this particular context.

I was using my friend's computer and could not get *the printer* to work.

❼ Using *the* to denote an entire class of things

The can be used with a singular count noun to denote an entire class or genre of things.

The earthworm is one of nature's most valuable creatures.

25c   Use *the* with most proper nouns derived from common nouns

Proper nouns are names of things such as persons, places, holidays, religions, companies, and organizations. Most proper nouns, even though they uniquely identify somebody or something, do not take the definite article:

Muhammad Ali   Mother Theresa   New York   Microsoft

Many proper nouns, though, do take the definite article:

the Rolling Stones   the United States
the Panama Canal   the International Red Cross

Those that take the definite article have a head noun derived from a common English noun: *stones, states, canal, cross*.

There are many exceptions, however, to this pattern: *Elm Street, Salt Lake City, Carleton College, Princeton University, Lookout Mountain*. We suggest that you pay close attention to each proper name you encounter and note whether it is used with *the*.

 Use *a* or *an* in nonspecific references to singular count nouns

Nonspecific nouns refer to *types* of things rather than to specific things. With nonspecific singular count nouns, such as *shirt, jacket, belt*, and *hat*, you must use an indefinite article (either *a* or, if the next sound is a vowel sound, *an*) or some other determiner (for example, *my, your, this*, or *each*).

I bought *a shirt* and *an overcoat*.

 In other cases, use no article

With nonspecific plural count nouns, such as *shirts, jackets, belts*, and *hats*, no article is used. You may use, however, determiners like *our, some, these*, and *no*.

There were *socks* and *shorts* on sale but *no belts*.

PHRASAL VERBS

Phrasal verbs are made up of a verb and one or two **particles** (prepositions or adverbs)—for example, *pick over, look into, get away with*. They are sometimes called two-word verbs or three-word verbs. Phrasal verbs are common in English, especially in informal speech. Some phrasal verbs mean something quite different from their associated simple verbs. For example, if a friend of yours says, "I just *ran into* Nguyen in the library," the encounter probably had nothing to do with running. *To run into* means "to encounter unintentionally." Other phrasal verbs are used merely to intensify the meaning of the simple verb. For example, *fill up* is a more emphatic version of *fill*.

Some phrasal verbs are **transitive** (that is, they have direct objects), while others are **intransitive**. For example, *dig up* (meaning "find") is transitive ("I *dug up* some information for my paper"), but *speak up* (meaning "speak louder") is intransitive ("Please *speak up*"). Some phrasal verbs have both transitive and intransitive meanings. For example, *show up* can mean either "expose or embarrass (someone)" or "arrive," depending on whether it is used transitively or intransitively. "He tried to *show up* the teacher" (transitive) versus "He never *shows up* on time" (intransitive).

Some transitive phrasal verbs are **separable**, meaning that the particle may be placed after the object of the verb: "I quickly *looked over* my paper" or "I quickly *looked* my paper *over*." Other transitive phrasal verbs are **inseparable**, meaning that the verb and the particle must be kept together: "I quickly *went over* my paper," not "I quickly *went* my paper *over*."

VERB COMPLEMENTS

Verb complements include gerunds (*swimming*), *to* infinitives (*to swim*), and unmarked infinitives (*swim*). English verbs differ in the kinds of verb complements they can take.

http://owl.english.purdue.edu/
handouts/grammar/g_verbals.html
Thorough coverage of verb
complements and verb tenses

>   V   Comp
> I *dislike swimming*. [Not "I dislike to swim" or "I dislike swim"]

>   V   Comp
> I *want to swim*. [Not "I want swimming" or "I want swim"]

>   V   Comp   V   Comp
> I *like swimming*. OR I *like to swim*. [Not "I like swim"]

>   V   Comp
> I *made* her *swim*. [Not "I made her swimming" or "I made her to swim"]

25f   Learn which verbs take -ing verb complements

The following verbs take gerunds (verbals ending in *-ing*), but not infinitives, as complements, as in "Maria *acknowledged skipping* class."

acknowledge	deny	give up	put off
admit	depend on	have trouble	quit
advise	detest	imagine	recommend
anticipate	discuss	insist on	regret
appreciate	dislike	keep	resist
avoid	dream about	miss	result in
cannot (can't) help	enjoy	object to	risk
consider	escape	plan on	succeed in
consist of	evade	postpone	suggest
delay	finish	practice	talk about

25g   Learn which verbs take to verb complements

The following verbs take *to* infinitives, but not participles, as complements, as in "Kim cannot *afford to buy* a car."

afford	consent	hesitate	manage	prepare	struggle
agree	decide	hope	mean	pretend	tend
ask	demand	intend	need	promise	threaten
attempt	expect	learn	offer	refuse	wait
claim	fail	like	plan	seem	want

25h   Learn which verbs take either -ing or to verb complements

The following verbs can take either a gerund or a *to* infinitive as a complement: "He *began learning* English as a small child" or "He *began to learn* English as a small child."

begin	dread	like	stop*
cannot (can't) stand	forget*	love	try
continue	hate	remember*	

For those verbs marked with an asterisk, the meaning of the sentence depends on the type of complement: "He *forgot to go* to the store" means that he did not go to the store, while "He *forgot going* to the store" means that he did go to the store but then did not remember going there.

 25i Learn the special properties of *have, help, let,* and *make*

Some verbs, when followed by a noun or pronoun, take an infinitive without *to* (an "unmarked" infinitive), as in "She *let him pay* for dinner." Such verbs include

> have   help   let   make

(Note that *help* can also take a *to* infinitive as a complement.)

VERBS OF STATE

Many English verbs depict states or conditions rather than events or actions. These verbs are called **verbs of state**.

 25j Do not use verbs of state like *understand* and *exist* in the *-ing* form

Verbs of state generally do not take on the progressive aspect. For example, *consist of* is a verb of state and therefore cannot occur in the progressive.

> *consists*
> The program ~~is consisting~~ of four parts.

The following verbs do not take on the progressive aspect:

appear	constitute	exist	need	seem
believe	contain	involve	possess	suppose
belong	correspond	know	represent	understand
consist of	differ from	mean	result in	want

MODAL AUXILIARY VERBS

The **modal auxiliary verbs** include *can, could, may, might, must, will, would,* and *should.* They are used to express a variety of conditions including possibility, necessity, ability, permission, and obligation. Each modal auxiliary has at least two principal meanings, one relating to social interaction and the other to logical probability. For example, the word *may* in a sentence like "*May I sit down?*" requests permission, an aspect of social interaction, while the word *may* in a sentence like "It *may* rain today" denotes logical possibility. Within these two general categories, the modal auxiliaries carry different degrees of strength. Modal auxiliary verbs have certain distinct grammatical features that can cause problems for nonnative speakers.

 25k Use only a base verb form immediately after a modal auxiliary

Any verb immediately following a modal auxiliary must be in the base, or simple, form (for example, *teach, have, go, run*), not in the *to* infinitive or gerund form.

NO   History *can to teach* us many good lessons.

YES   History *can teach* us many good lessons.

 25l Do not use more than one modal at a time

NO   If I study hard, I *might could* get an A.

YES   If I study hard, I *might* get an A.

YES   If I study hard, I *could* get an A.

If you want to combine a modal auxiliary verb with some other modal meaning, use a modal phrase such as *be able to, be allowed to,* or *have to.*

YES   If I study hard, I *might be able to* get an A.

CONDITIONAL SENTENCES

Conditional sentences have two parts: a subordinate clause beginning with *if* (or *when* or *unless*) that sets a condition and a main clause that expresses a result. The tense and mood of the verb in the subordinate clause depend on the tense and mood of the verb in the main clause. There are three main types of conditional sentences: factual, predictive, and hypothetical.

25m In factual conditionals, use the same verb tense in both parts

Factual conditional sentences describe factual relationships. The conditional clause begins with *if, when, whenever,* or some other condition-setting expression; the conditional clause verb is cast in the same tense as the result clause verb.

If you don't *get* enough rest, you *get* tired.

25n In predictive conditionals, use a present-tense verb in the *if* clause and an appropriate modal in the result clause

Predictive conditional sentences express future possible conditions and results. The conditional clause starts with *if* or *unless* and has a present-tense verb; the result clause verb is formed with a modal (*will, can, should, may,* or *might*) and the base form of the verb.

If we *leave* now, we *can be* there by five o'clock.

25o In hypothetical conditionals, use a past-tense verb in the *if* clause and *would, could,* or *might* in the result clause

Hypothetical conditional sentences describe situations that are unlikely to happen or are contrary to fact. For hypothetical past situations, the verb in the conditional clause should be in the past perfect tense and the verb in the main clause should be formed from *would have, could have,* or *might have* and the past participle.

If we *had invested* our money in stocks instead of bonds, we *would have gained* a lot more.

For hypothetical present or future situations, the verb in the conditional clause should be in the past tense and the verb in the main clause should be formed from *would, could*, or *might* and the base form.

If we *invested* our money in stocks instead of bonds, we *would gain* a lot more.

TIPS ON WORD ORDER

Unlike many other languages, English depends on word order to convey meaning. A change in word order often produces a different meaning. For example, "Kevin likes Maria" means something quite different from "Maria likes Kevin." This section discusses word-order patterns involving strings of adjectives, compound nouns, and adverb placement.

 25p String adjectives in the order preferred in English

If you string two or more adjectives together, you have to put them in the appropriate order.

FAULTY   The *wood broken* fence will be repaired.

REVISED   The *broken wood* fence will be repaired.

The following list shows the preferred order of adjectives in English:

1. Article or determiner: *the, a, an, my, our, Carla's, this, that, those*
2. Ordinal expression: *first, second, last, next, final*
3. Quantity: *one, two, few, many, some*
4. Evaluation: *beautiful, delicious, interesting, unfortunate, ugly*
5. Size: *tiny, small, short, tall, large, big*
6. Shape: *square, oval, cylindrical, round*
7. Condition: *shiny, clean, dirty, broken*
8. Age: *new, young, old, ancient*

9. Color: *black, red, yellow, green, white*
10. Nationality: *Mexican, Chinese, Vietnamese, Japanese*
11. Religion: *Catholic, Confucian, Buddhist, Muslim*
12. Material: *cotton, stone, plastic, gold*
13. Special use or purpose (may be a noun used as an adjective): *carving, carrying, sports, medical, computer*
14. The noun being modified

Here are some expressions created by following the preferred ordering:

1	2	3	4	5	6	7	8	9	10	11	12	13	14
The	first			small		shiny	new		Japanese			sports	car
A	few						young			Buddhist			monks
Her			favorite	long				yellow			silk		flowers

25q String nouns for easiest recognition

Stringing nouns together to form noun compounds is common in English. Terms like *bike lock, keyboard, houseboat, picnic table*, and *bookmark* were formed by putting two ordinary nouns together. And it is easy to add a third noun to make them more descriptive: *combination bike lock, keyboard cover, houseboat community, picnic table leg*, and *bookmark program*.

In all noun compounds, the rightmost noun is the head noun and the nouns preceding it serve as modifiers. These modifier nouns can modify either the head noun or another modifier noun.

Nouns used as modifiers typically lose any plural endings they might have. Someone who loves movies is a *movie lover*, not a *movies lover*; the juice from cranberries is *cranberry juice*, not *cranberries juice*.

25r   Use meaning to place adverbs that modify verbs

Adverbs can modify verbs, adjectives, other adverbs, or entire sentences. Adverbs that modify verbs can be placed at either the beginning, the middle, or the end of a clause, depending on their meaning.

❶ Placing adverbs of frequency

Adverbs of frequency (*usually, seldom, always, never*) are usually placed directly before the main verb (and after the auxiliary verb, if there is one).

> Tim says he *usually* writes his papers on time, yet he is *always* turning them in late.

Some adverbs of frequency (*often, twice, many times*) can also be placed at the end of the clause.

> He has missed class *quite often*.

❷ Placing adverbs of time

Adverbs of time of occurrence (*yesterday, at eight o'clock, last year*) are normally placed at the end of the clause.

> The exhibit will open *next month*.

❸ Placing adverbs of place

Adverbs of place (*upstairs, in the park, under a tree*) usually follow the verb. However, they should not intervene between the verb and an object.

> She took her dog for a walk *in the park*.

25s   Place adverbs directly before adjectives or adverbs that they modify

An adverb that modifies an adjective or another adverb should be placed directly before the word it modifies.

> Jose is an *unusually quick* learner. He concentrates *very intensely* on his studies.

25t Place adverbs before sentences or clauses that they modify

An adverb that modifies a whole sentence or clause is usually placed at the beginning of the sentence or clause.

> *Unfortunately*, his younger brother Ramon does not follow his example.

 25u Do not put an adverb between a verb and its object

Nonnative speakers sometimes make the mistake of positioning an adverb between the verb and its object or objects.

FAULTY   Javier writes *often* letters to his family.

REVISED   Javier *often* writes letters to his family.

TIPS ON VOCABULARY

Many nonnative speakers of English feel that they just do not know enough words to express their thoughts as fully as they would like. This section covers some of the most common vocabulary problems for nonnative speakers—those related to cognates, collocations, and idioms.

 25v Look for cognates, but watch out for "false friends"

Cognates are words that have a formal relation to similar words in another language. They are usually quite recognizable. For example, the English *telephone* and Spanish *teléfono* are cognates, and it is easy for speakers of either language to recognize this word when learning the other language.

If your native language is closely related to English, cognate recognition is a good strategy for learning new words. In most cases, you can trust a cognate to carry more or less the same meaning in your second language as it has in your first language. Of course, there are often subtle differences that you should pay attention to. For example, although the word *collar* is used in both

English and Spanish to refer to the band around the neck of an animal, in Spanish it is also used to mean "necklace."

Sometimes, however, words that look similar in two different languages have entirely different meanings. These words are called **false cognates** or false friends. An example of a false cognate is the English *jubilation* and Spanish *jubilación*. The English word means "happiness," while the Spanish one means "retirement, pension (money)." You should always be on the alert for false cognates. Never assume that two words mean the same thing just because they look similar.

 Try to get a feel for collocations

Collocations are words that commonly occur together. For example, the word *advice* commonly occurs with the verbs *give, get,* and *receive* and with the adjectives *good, bad,* and *sound*. This is why the sentence "She gave me some good advice" sounds like normal American English, while the sentence "She presented me some nice advice" does not.

>   *rise*
> A steep ~~upshoot~~ in grain prices could topple many governments in the Third World.

>   *broad*
> Lazy thinkers tend to make ~~wide~~ generalizations about things.

The best way to develop your knowledge of collocations is to pay attention to them in the English you see and hear around you. In this way, you will develop a feel for which words go with which.

 Learn idioms in their entirety

A special type of collocation is the **idiomatic expression**, or **idiom**. An idiom is a fixed phrase that has its own special meaning. For example, *kick the bucket* is an idiom that means "die"; it has nothing to do with either kicking or buckets (pails). The same holds true for other idioms, such as *beat around the bush,*

have a screw loose, or *lip service*, which have nothing to do with bushes, screws, or lips. Because idioms are so special and unpredictable, you have to learn them one at a time, in their entirety. And you have to use them in exactly the right form. If you said *kick a bucket* or *kick the pail*, many listeners would not understand what you meant. Many idioms involve phrasal verbs.

The best way to learn a language's idioms is by listening to native speakers. Some good Web sites can also be of help: Dave Sperling's Idiom Page at *http://www.pacificnet.net/~sperling/idioms.cgi*, Vocabulary on the Internet at *http://ec.hku.hk/vec/vocab/vocint.htm*, and English Daily at *http://www.englishdaily626.com/idioms.php* are especially reliable.

Glossary of Usage

a, an   Use *a* before words beginning with a consonant sound: *a program, a uniform*. Use *an* before words beginning with a vowel sound: *an open book, an uncle*.

accept, except   *Accept* is a verb meaning "receive gladly." *Except* is usually a preposition meaning "excluding."

adapt, adopt   *Adapt* means "adjust" or "make suitable." *Adopt* means "take as one's own." *If you adopt a child, you will have to adapt to it.*

advice, advise   *Advice* is a noun meaning "guidance." *Advise* is a verb meaning "guide." *I advised her to take my advice.*

affect, effect   *Affect* is usually a verb meaning "influence": *Bad weather seems to affect my mood. Effect* is usually a noun meaning "result." As a verb, *effect* means "bring about": *The new policy will effect important changes.*

aggravate   "Make worse." *Donna's asthma was aggravated by the polluted air.* Commonly used also to mean "irritate," though some experts consider this incorrect.

ain't   Nonstandard. *Am not, is not, are not,* and *have not* are preferred in standard English.

all ready, already   *All ready* is an adjective phrase meaning "prepared": *They were all ready to go. Already* is an adverb meaning "by this time": *They have already left.*

all right   Should be spelled as two words. An adjective phrase meaning "satisfactory."

all together, altogether   *All together* means "in unison; as a group." *Altogether* means "completely." *The witnesses spoke out all together. They were altogether happy to get the chance.*

a lot   Spelled as two words, not *alot* or *allot*. Informal. In formal writing, use *much* or *many* instead.

among, between   See *between, among.*

and etc.   Redundant; use *etc.* or *and so on.*

anxious, eager   *Anxious* means "uneasy, worried": *We were anxious about the weather*. *Eager* means "having a strong desire": *We were eager to see the show*.

anymore   Should be used only in negative sentences: *She doesn't live here anymore*. In positive sentences, use *nowadays*. *I have many friends nowadays* (not *anymore*).

anyways, anywheres   Nonstandard for *anyway* and *anywhere*.

as, like   See *like, as*.

at   Redundant when used with *where*: The colloquial *Where is he at?* should be shortened in formal writing to *Where is he?*

at this point in time   Wordy. Use *now, at present*, or *currently*.

awful, awfully   Avoid using these words to mean "very," except in informal communication.

bad, badly   *Bad* is an adjective and *badly* is an adverb; avoid mixing these functions, as in "*I feel badly*" or "*He plays bad*."

because of, due to   Use *because of* after a clause: *She had a headache because of stress*. Use *due to* after a noun: *Her headache was due to stress*.

being as, being that   These phrases are colloquial when used in sentences like *Being as the roads are icy, we should drive carefully*. In formal writing, replace them with *because* or *since*.

better, had better   *Had better* is an idiomatic expression meaning "should": *You had better leave*. It is acceptable in formal writing. *You better leave* is too colloquial.

between, among   Use *between* when referring to distinct individuals, especially two of them: *Let's divide it up between you and me*. Use *among* when referring to a mass or collectivity: *Let's divide it up among our friends*.

bring, take   *Bring* suggests motion toward the writer or speaker; *take* suggests motion away from the writer or speaker. *You bring something here, but you take something there*.

but   May be used to begin a sentence. Some traditionalists, however, disagree with such usage.

calculate, figure, reckon   Colloquial expressions for "guess" or "suppose," as in *I calculate we'll have a losing season again*. In formal writing, use *suppose, surmise*, or *imagine*.

can, may *Can* is preferred when expressing ability, *may* is preferred when requesting permission: *May* (not *can*) *I have another piece? Can* (not *may*) *she walk without crutches?*

can't hardly, can't scarcely Nonstandard. In formal writing, use *can hardly* or *can scarcely*: *Even accountants can hardly make sense of the tax code.*

center around In formal writing, *center on* is preferred. *My paper will center on hate speech.*

cite, site *Cite* is a verb meaning "name or quote." *Site* is a noun meaning "place."

climactic, climatic *Climactic* is the adjective form of *climax*: *King Lear's death is the climactic event of the play. Climatic* is the adjective form of *climate*: *Global warming could be a climatic disaster.*

complement, compliment A *complement* is something that completes a whole: *The flowers beautifully complemented the table setting.* A *compliment* is an expression of praise: *She complimented me on my dancing.*

compose, comprise *Compose* means "make up, constitute." *Comprise* means "consist of." *Seven days compose one week; one week comprises seven days.*

conscience, conscious *Conscience* is a noun meaning "a sense of right and wrong." *Conscious* is an adjective meaning "aware" or "intentional": *Todd made a conscious decision to clear his guilty conscience.*

continual, continuous *Continual* means "repeated at intervals." *Continuous* means "without interruption." The flow of time is *continuous*, but a heartbeat is *continual.*

could of Nonstandard for *could have. He could have tried harder.*

council, counsel A *council* is an assembly of people who advise or regulate. *Counsel* means "advice or guidance." *A council can give counsel.*

criterion, criteria *Criterion* is singular, meaning "standard of judgment." *Criteria* is the plural form.

data Traditionally, *data* was used only as the plural form of *datum*. However, it is now also (and more commonly) used as a singular form meaning "numerical information."

device, devise *Device* is a noun meaning "small machine" or "scheme." *Devise* is a verb meaning "plan or invent."

different from, different than In formal writing, use *different from* when the comparison is between two persons or things: *My opinion is different from* *hers*. Use *different than* when the object of comparison is a full clause: *The party turned out <u>different than</u> I wanted it to be.*

disinterested, uninterested   *Disinterested* means "neutral, unbiased." *Uninterested* means "unconcerned, indifferent to." *Although good judges are always <u>disinterested</u> in the case before them, they are not likely to be <u>uninterested</u> in it.*

due to   See *because of, due to.*

effect   See *affect, effect.*

emigrate, immigrate, migrate   *Emigrate* means "move permanently away from." *Immigrate* means "move permanently to." *Migrate* means "move temporarily from one place to another."

eminent, immanent, imminent   *Eminent* means "distinguished": *She is an <u>eminent</u> scholar. Immanent* means "inherent": *God's spirit is <u>immanent</u> in nature. Imminent* means "about to occur": *A stock market crash is <u>imminent</u>.*

enthused   As an adjective, *enthused* is nonstandard. In formal writing, use *enthusiastic.*

especially, specially   *Especially* means "deserving of special emphasis; particularly." *I am <u>especially</u> happy about my math grade. Specially* is the adverb form of *special*; it means "exceptionally" or "for a particular reason." *Today is a <u>specially</u> designated holiday.*

et al.   Abbreviation for Latin *et alii* ("and others"). Should be used only to avoid repeated reference to three or more authors of a single work. *Johnson <u>et al.</u> make the same argument.*

etc.   Abbreviation for Latin *et cetera* ("and the rest"). Should not refer to people and should not be used in formal writing. Instead of *She likes Picasso, Van Gogh, etc.,* write *She likes such artists as Picasso and Van Gogh* or *She likes Picasso, Van Gogh, and other such artists.*

everyone, every one   *Everyone* is an indefinite pronoun: *Everyone is here.* In *every one, one* is a pronoun and *every* is a quantifier: *<u>Every one</u> of the guests has been seated.*

except, accept   See *accept, except.*

expect   Verb meaning "anticipate." In formal writing, should not be used to mean "presume" or "suppose": *I <u>suppose</u>* (not *expect*) *you're right.*

farther, further   *Farther* refers to distance: *She hit the ball <u>farther</u> than anyone else. Further* refers to time or degree: *Should we go <u>further</u> with our research?*

fewer, less Use *fewer* with items that can be counted. Use *less* with general amounts. *He had fewer problems and less anxiety than I did.*

figure See *calculate, figure, reckon.*

firstly, secondly, thirdly Common in British English but sounds pretentious in American English. Use *first, second, third.*

get Informal in most uses, especially idiomatic expressions like *get cracking* or *get around to.* In some cases, your thesaurus will suggest more formal alternatives.

good, well *Good* is an adjective; *well* is an adverb: *I feel good. I write well.*

gorilla, guerrilla A *gorilla* is a large ape. A *guerrilla* is a member of a rebel army.

hanged, hung Use *hanged* for executions, *hung* for all other past-tense meanings. *The prisoner was hanged at dawn. The flag was hung from the railing.*

hardly, scarcely These adverbs have a negative meaning ("almost not at all"); using them with *not* creates a double negative, which is nonstandard in English. Instead, omit the *not*: *It hardly matters* (not *It doesn't hardly matter*).

he, him, his Using this singular masculine pronoun generically—that is, to refer to a mixed-gender group of people—is considered sexist by many.

he/she, him/her, his/her These forms can be used to avoid the sexism of generic *he, him,* or *his.* Use them sparingly, however.

heard, herd *Heard* is the past form of *hear.* *Herd* is a group of animals.

hisself Nonstandard for *himself.* *He shot himself* (not *hisself*) *in the foot.*

hole, whole *Hole* is a noun meaning "gap" or "cavity." *Whole* is an adjective meaning "complete" or "entire."

hopefully Used widely as a sentence adverb, as in *Hopefully, the war will soon be over.* Although this usage is grammatically correct, some readers object to it.

if, whether Although both of these conjunctions can be used to express an alternative, *whether* is clearer. *She doesn't know whether she can go.*

immigrate See *emigrate.*

imply, infer *Imply* means "suggest indirectly." *Infer* means "draw a conclusion from what someone else has said." *The owner implied that I didn't have enough experience; I inferred that she would not offer me the job.*

incredible, incredulous *Incredible* means "unbelievable": *His performance was incredible. Incredulous* means "disbelieving": *He was incredulous when he heard the news.*

individual, person *Individual* is overused as a substitute for *person*. *Individual* should be reserved for situations emphasizing a person's distinctiveness: *Elizabeth Cady Stanton was a remarkable individual*. *Person* can be used in all other cases: *The person (not individual) who stole my laptop will be caught sooner or later*.

ingenious, ingenuous *Ingenious* means "inventive, clever"; *ingenuous* means "unsophisticated, candid."

in regards to Nonstandard. Use *in regard to* or *regarding* or *as regards*.

instill, install *Instill* means "implant," as in *A good parent instills good character in a child*. *Install* means "set in position for use," as in *I should install new brakes in my car*.

irregardless Nonstandard for *regardless*.

its, it's *Its* is the possessive form of *it*. *It's* is the contracted form of *it is*. *It's important that a company give its employees a sense of security*.

kind of, sort of, type of Be careful to observe number agreement with these modifiers. Use *this kind of book* (all singular) or *these kinds of books* (all plural), not *"these kind of books," "these kinds of book,"* or *"this kind of books."*

lay, lie *Lay* takes a direct object: *They want to lay a wreath at his grave*. *Lie* does not take a direct object: *I think I'll lie down for a while*.

lead, led *Lead* is a noun referring to a certain type of metal. *Led* is the past form of the verb *lead*: *Our efforts have led to nothing*.

leave, let *Leave* means "go away": *She plans to leave tomorrow*. *Let* means "allow": *Let me pay for this*.

lend, loan These verbs both mean "give something temporarily." But *loan* is used only for monetary transactions, while *lend* can be used for more figurative meanings, such as *lend someone a hand*.

less, fewer See *fewer, less*.

lie, lay See *lay, lie*.

like, as In formal writing, use *like* as a preposition before a noun phrase and *as* as a conjunction before a clause: *She looked like her mother* vs. *She looked as I thought she would*.

lose, loose *Lose* is a verb meaning "fail to keep." *Loose* is an adjective meaning "not fastened."

lots Informal. Use *many* or *much*.

man, mankind   Avoid these terms in situations where gender-inclusive terms like *people, humanity, humans, humankind,* or *men and women* can be used instead.

may   See *can, may.*

might of   Nonstandard for *might have. They might have* (not *might of*) *left.*

moral, morale   A *moral* is a lesson taught in a story. *Morale* is a state of mind regarding confidence and cheerfulness.

must of   Nonstandard for *must have. They must have* (not *must of*) *lost their way.*

okay, OK   Informal. In formal writing, use more precise terms like *enjoyable, acceptable,* or *pleasing.*

personal, personnel   *Personal* is an adjective meaning "private" or "individual." *Personnel* is a noun meaning the people employed by an organization. *The personnel office keeps personal files on all the company's employees.*

phenomenon, phenomena   A *phenomenon* is "a perceivable occurrence or fact." *Phenomena* is the plural form.

plus   Colloquial when used in place of *moreover: We had gone past the deadline; moreover* (not *plus*), *we were over budget.*

precede, proceed   *Precede* means "come before"; *proceed* means "go ahead."

pretty   In formal writing, avoid using *pretty* as an adverb. *Hemingway was a very* (not *pretty*) *good writer.*

principal, principle   *Principal* is an adjective meaning "foremost." *Principle* is a noun meaning "rule" or "standard." *Our principal concern is to maintain our high principles.*

raise, rise   *Raise* is a transitive verb meaning "lift" or "build": *He raised his hand. Rise* is an intransitive verb meaning "stand up" or "ascend": *She rose from her chair.*

real, really   *Real* is an adjective; *really* is an adverb. In most cases, both of these terms should be avoided in formal writing. *The economy is doing very* (not *real* or *really*) *well.*

reason . . . is because   Colloquial. Use *reason . . . is that* in formal writing. *The reason the Yankees won is that they had better pitching.*

respectfully, respectively   *Respectfully* means "with respect." *Respectively* means "in the order given." *The teacher called on Bart and Juana, respectively.*

set, sit *Set* is used most often as a transitive verb meaning "place" or "arrange": *Set the table. Sit* is an intransitive verb meaning "take a seat": *Sit down over here.*

shall, will In American English, *shall* is used for polite questions in the first person (*Shall we sit down?*) and in highly formal or legalistic writing. Otherwise, *will* is the standard helping verb for future tenses.

should of Nonstandard for *should have.*

somewheres Nonstandard for *somewhere.*

sort of See *kind of, sort of, type of.*

specially See *especially, specially.*

stationary, stationery *Stationary* is an adjective meaning "not moving." *Stationery* is a noun meaning "writing paper."

take, bring See *bring, take.*

than, then *Than* is a conjunction used to introduce the second part of a comparison: *Donna is taller than Jo. Then* is an adverb meaning "at that time" or "next."

that, which As a relative pronoun, *that* is used only in essential clauses: *The storm that* (or *which*) *everyone talks about occurred ten years ago. Which* can be used with either essential or nonessential clauses: *The storm of 2004, which I'll never forget, destroyed part of our roof.*

their, there, they're *Their* is the possessive form of *they: They retrieved their car. There* is an adverb of place; it is also used in expletive constructions: *There is someone at the door. They're* is a contraction of *they are: They're too young to drive.*

theirselves Nonstandard. Use *themselves.*

threw, through/thru *Threw* is the past form of the verb *throw. Through* is a preposition, as in "walk through the house." Do not use *thru* in formal writing.

till, until, 'til *Till* and *until* are both acceptable in formal writing. *'Til* is informal.

type of See *kind of, sort of, type of.*

unique "The only one of its kind." In formal English, *unique* should be used without any degree modification. *Tiger Woods is a unique* (not *very unique*) *athlete.*

until See *till, until, 'til.*

use, utilize   In most cases, *use* is the better choice. *Utilize* means "make practical use of" and should be used only with this meaning.

weak, week   *Weak* is the opposite of *strong*. *Week* is a period of seven days.

weather, whether   *Weather* is a noun meaning "atmospheric conditions." *Whether* is a conjunction meaning "if."

which, that   See *that, which*.

who, whom   *Who* and *whom* are used as interrogative or relative pronouns. *Who* stands for a grammatical subject; *whom* stands for a grammatical object.

who's, whose   *Who's* is a contraction for *who is*. *Whose* is the possessive form of *who*.

would have   Should not be used in the *if* part of a conditional sentence. *If I had* (not *would have*) *started sooner, I would have finished the paper on time.*

would of   Nonstandard for *would have*.

your, you're   *Your* is the possessive form of *you*. *You're* is a contraction of *you are*. *You're loyal to your friends.*

Index